RUNIC

PALMISTRY

What Secrets Do You Hold in Your Hands?

In palmistry, every detail of the hand has meaning. We consider the relationships between the fingers, the lines on the hands, the skin ridge patterns, the temperature and ruddiness of the skin, and even the hair pattern and skin texture. Some palmists believe that there are no such things as accidents and even scars and injuries to the hand may have special meanings.

The first thing I suggest you notice is the shape of the hand. This provides a clue to the person's instinctive reactions to life. For example, round hands tend to be feelers and creators; square hands are thinkers and planners, and so on. Don't worry about trying to remember this right now. I'll go into more detail in chapter 3.

After determining the shape of the hand, you're ready to move on to the fingers. Fingers reveal how people manipulate the world around them. Each finger has a different meaning, which we'll examine in more detail in chapters 4 and 5.

Next you will begin to interpret the branches and mounts in the hands. This will allow you to fine-tune the reading to razor-point accuracy. We'll look at this closely in chapters 6 and 7.

And finally, you'll locate the palm runes and interpret them. This exciting procedure will be touched on in the second half of this book, along with two simple methods of runecasts.

You are about to embark on a wonderful journey of self-discovery. I hope you'll find the trip as fascinating as I have.

Jon Saint-Germain

About the Author

When he was six years old, Jon Saint-Germain learned to read palms from his grandmother. He has been a lifelong student of the craft ever since. Jon has been a professional psychic entertainer and palm reader for over twenty years. He is a popular lecturer on palmistry, and his show "MindBenders" takes him across the country. Jon has written thirteen books on psychic subjects and the psychology of entertainment. In 1997 he was awarded the Blackwood Award by the Psychic Entertainer's Association for his contributions to the literatures of mentalism. He lives in Knoxville, Tennessee, with his wife, Elizabeth, and three cats, Oliver, Boo, and Emma.

To Write to the Author

If you wish to contact the author or would like more information about this book, please write to the author in care of Llewellyn Worldwide and we will forward your request. Both the author and publisher appreciate hearing from you and learning of your enjoyment of this book and how it has helped you. Llewellyn Worldwide cannot guarantee that every letter written to the author can be answered, but all will be forwarded. Please write to:

Jon Saint-Germain
℅ Llewellyn Worldwide
P.O. Box 64383, Dept. 1-56718-577-0
St. Paul, MN 55164-0383, U.S.A.
Please enclose a self-addressed stamped envelope for reply,
or $1.00 to cover costs. If outside U.S.A., enclose
international postal reply coupon.

Many of Llewellyn's authors have websites with additional information and resources. For more information, please visit our website at
http://www.llewellyn.com

RUNIC PALMISTRY

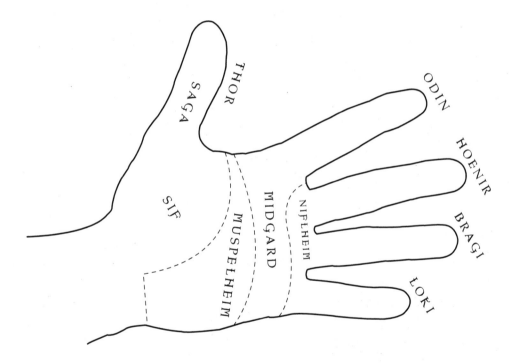

JON SAINT-GERMAIN

2001
Llewellyn Publications
St. Paul, Minnesota 55164-0383, U.S.A.

First Edition
First Printing, 2001

Book design and editing by Joanna Willis
Cover design by Kevin R. Brown
Cover background photo © Digital Stock
Interior illustrations by Gavin Dayton Duffy, Llewellyn Worldwide

Library of Congress Cataloging-in-Publication Data
Runic palmistry / Jon Saint-Germain.
    p.   cm.
Includes bibliographical references and index.
ISBN 1-56718-577-0
  1. Palmistry. 2. Mythology, Norse. 3. Runes. I. Title.

BF921 .S22 2001
133.6—dc21

2001029278

Llewellyn Worldwide does not participate in, endorse, or have any authority or responsibility concerning private business transactions between our authors and the public.

All mail addressed to the author is forwarded but the publisher cannot, unless specifically instructed by the author, give out an address or phone number.

Any Internet references contained in this work are current at publication time, but the publisher cannot guarantee that a specific location will continue to be maintained. Please refer to the publisher's website for links to authors' websites and other sources.

Llewellyn Publications
A Division of Llewellyn Worldwide, Ltd.
P.O. Box 64383, Dept. 1-56718-577-0
St. Paul, MN 55164-0383, USA
www.llewellyn.com

 Printed in the United States of America on recycled paper

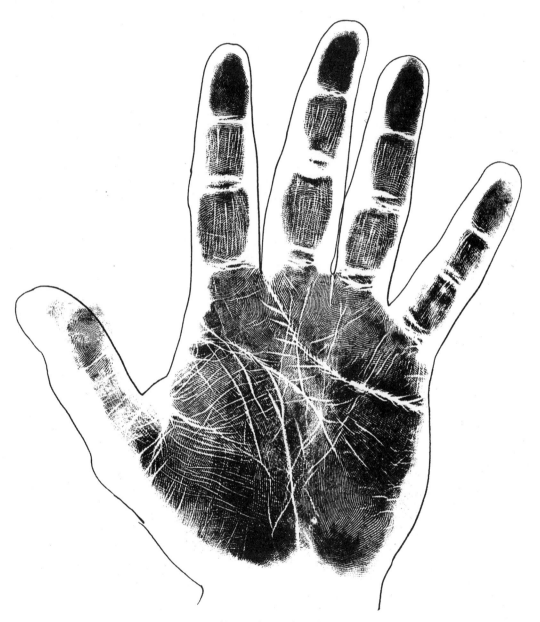

The author's hand

CONTENTS

PART I
Reading the Hand

PART II
The Runes

FOREWORD

New palmistry books usually struggle with the basic problems of learning and utilizing palmistry. The fundamental questions are reexamined, rediscussed, and reevaluated. Basic questions are revived but very little new information is presented.

Not so in Jon Saint-Germain's book *Runic Palmistry*. Jon has combined the oral legacy of the rune alphabet with the physical hand markings familiar to palmistry. The word *rune* means "a secret" or "to whisper." The beginnings of this arcane system have been lost in the mists of time. What has come down to us has been transmitted orally to John through his mother and grandmother.

Presented in this book are concepts that will be new to most people who have studied palmistry. Jon's vast knowledge of the Teutonic races that developed the rune alphabet combined with the Norse/Irish stories of his grandmother have come together to produce a major breakthrough in the new material written about palmistry.

In general, psychologists have been quick to dismiss the art of palmistry. Yet when Carl Jung—a psychologist whose work is widely accepted today—wrote about alchemy (an art only half as old as palmistry), he stated, "When an idea is so old and so generally believed, it must be true in some way, by which I mean that it is psychologically true." Too often psychologists have taken the position that there was no heat before the thermometer!

You have in your hands a book that will give you a thorough insight into the "whisper of others" with only a glimpse of their hand. I hope you enjoy this book as much as I have.

FRED CROUTER
Psychologist

PREFACE

These things are thought the best:
Fire, the sight of the sun,
Good health with the gift to keep it,
And a life that avoids vice.

THE WORDS OF THE HIGH ONE,
AN ANCIENT NORSE POEM

Palmistry has been my passion since I was about six years old. Practically everyone on my mother's side of the family reads palms, but I'm one of the very few males in the family who took an interest in the craft. This is probably because I was raised by both my mother and grandmother who encouraged me to develop my psychic abilities.

My mother was good, but Grandma was without a doubt the best psychic I had ever seen. She had a way of sugarcoating bad news and putting such a positive spin on people's negative traits that people didn't know when they were being chewed out! She strongly influenced my decision to become a professional palm reader. If it hadn't been for her, I probably never would have gotten into this strange business to start with.

As a child I was constantly encouraged to study and develop my intuitive abilities. I even had my own dog-eared pack of Tarot cards, and Grandma spent countless hours telling me little stories about the people on them. But mainly she taught me about the language of the hand.

I remember when Grandma first took my small (and probably dirty) hand in hers and traced with her forefinger the formation where the life line, heart line, and fate line intersected to form the letter *M* in my palm. "You see that, Jonny?" she said, her voice lilting with just a shade of an Irish accent. "That *M* means you're an old soul in a young body."

"What's that mean, Mamaw?" I turned my hand every which way trying to make out what she was showing me.

She laughed. "It means that you'll grow up and be a psychic, baby. You will have an understanding of people and a sympathetic nature. You'll help people and make lots of money doing it." (She later told me that the letter was an *M* for "Magician" or a *W* for "Witch," depending on how they tied you to the stake back in the bad old days.)

Grandma was always right. About ten years ago I finally made the decision to become a professional psychic reader. I've used runic palmistry, just as she taught me, to help literally thousands of people with their problems. (But I have yet to make a lot of money doing it! I'm just too easy, I guess.)

The Search Begins

If you've never heard of runic palmistry before, you're not alone. Except for a fortunate twist of fate, the technique would have been lost to the world almost two hundred years ago!

Let me explain. Until the early 1980s, everything I knew about palmistry I learned from my grandmother. Up to that time it never occurred to me that there was any other way to read hands. Only after I began to meet other palmists did I realize that Grandma's methods were different from everyone else's. For example, she always called the lines in the palm "branches" and had unusual names for the fingers. Most of these names were derived from Norse mythology—a curious thing in itself, since my grandmother's family came from Ireland!

My curiosity aroused, I began collecting and studying books on palm reading. What an eye-opening experience! After searching through several hundred books on the subject, I realized that my grandmother had learned palmistry from an entirely different source than any I could locate—but where?

I Become an Historian

Knowing that the techniques and traditions I had learned had been passed down in my family for generations, I became very curious about the origins of our unusual palmistry system. I remembered the stories my grandmother told about the Norse gods and heroes, but where had she learned them? Unfortunately, Grandma had passed away years before and could not answer my questions.

I didn't have to wait very long for answers. The first clues came from my grandma's younger sister, Great-Aunt Eliza. In 1985 I traveled to Bull's Gap, Tennessee, and spent a few days with her. Great-Aunt Eliza could have been the subject of a book all by herself. She was quite eccentric and at the age of ninety-four still hauled her own water from a well, cut firewood, and dug coal for her stove! Trying to keep up with her almost exhausted me.

During a rare moment of rest I quizzed Aunt Eliza about the family's style of palmistry and where it came from. Sipping her homemade tea, she told me that it had all started in Ireland. Her great-grandmother Aileen had learned to read palms from her lover, a Scandinavian named Sigurd. "What he was doing in Ireland is anybody's guess," Aunt Eliza cackled. "Probably running from the law," she conjectured. I was intrigued by the possibility that my family had learned to read palms from a Scandinavian outlaw!

Great-Great-Grandmother Aileen had taught the method to her daughter and granddaughters (my grandmother and Eliza), who in turn taught it to my mother and to me. Aunt Eliza was an extraordinary palmist with an almost legendary reputation and a nearly photographic memory. She remembered everything she had ever learned. In between chopping wood, patching the roof, and clearing away brush, I managed to record pages of information about the system. I returned home, and after applying ice to my aching body, began work on my notes.

Sigurd or Siglinde?

My mother added more anecdotes to the legend. Looking over my notes, she corrected me on one point: "You say here that she learned to read palms from someone named Sigurd. That's not right. Mama said Aileen learned it from her governess whose name was Siglinde." Subsequent investigation revealed a fifty-fifty split in my family about the sex of the mysterious Scandinavian palmist. Was the name Sigurd or Siglinde? My great-uncle Vonduss remembered the name "Sigfried." Another family tradition suggested that Sigurd or Siglinde had been in telepathic communication with ancient Viking and Druid seers who taught him or her the secrets of palmistry. Most believed that the Scandinavian, whoever he or she was, had fled to Ireland to evade the law.

Who can separate myth from fact? Was the name changed from the male *Sigurd* to the female *Siglinde* to protect Great-Great-Granny Aileen's memory from scandal in those conservative days? Who knows? All I knew for sure was that my family possessed a hitherto unknown method of reading palms based on ancient Norse divination techniques. The origins of this system appeared to be lost in the mists of time. Since I couldn't find any reference to the Norse palmistry system anywhere else, I decided to take the scraps of information and record them before they were lost forever. You are holding the results in your hands.

The Next Step: Palm Runes

When runestones (an ancient Norse method of divination) became available to the public, I began incorporating runecasts into Norse palmistry readings. The two seemed to go hand in hand, so I gave a set of runestones to Aunt Eliza for her ninety-sixth birthday. She seemed delighted with her new toys and immediately threw herself into studying them.

A few months later I received a letter from Aunt Eliza containing many pages of notes and drawings. She had discovered the runic symbols could be found in the palm of the hand itself! This breakthrough came as a natural evolution of the family tradition. The last piece had fallen into place.

Thanks to Aunt Eliza's observation I've seen that almost everyone has runes hidden in their hands. The runes in the palm seem to provide wonderful insights and often suggest solutions to long-standing problems. We will learn the meaning of these runes in Part II of this book.

Did the Vikings Practice Palmistry?

Although there are no surviving records proving that Norse seers practiced palmistry, legend tells us that special marks on the fingernails called *Nornaspor* ("Norn's Spurs") were considered signs of good fortune. This suggests that Norsemen must have studied their hands at some point in history. Unfortunately, early Christian missionaries destroyed every bit of information they could find about the "pagan" Norse religion, so we cannot determine if Norsemen practiced palmistry or not. Although it seems likely they did, we just don't know for sure. Where and how the Scandinavian outlaw Sigurd/Siglinde learned to read palms is still an unanswered question.

Completing the Picture

The most exciting aspect of runic palmistry is that it can be combined with a runecast. The two procedures compliment each other and provide a complete picture of the client's past, present, and future. If you already have some knowledge of classical palmistry or rune reading, you'll pick up the additional information very quickly. Even if you're a newcomer to these methods, don't let your inexperience daunt you. It's not all that difficult.

A Different Perspective

I cannot take any credit for the system of runic palmistry described in this book. All I have done is collect the information from my family's memories and compared it with existing historical sources. The original information was passed on to my family by the mysterious Sigurd or Siglinde around 180 years ago and I've tried to record it as faithfully as possible. But as with any oral tradition, some inaccuracies are bound to occur and I would be a poor scribe indeed if I allowed the errors to stand uncorrected. For instance, the area of the hand ruled by Sif (Thor's wife) had been called "Siffy" by both my grandmother and Great-Aunt Eliza. Thor himself, Lord of Thunder, was called "Thorn." I've corrected the pronunciations wherever necessary.

Final Thoughts

I suggest you study other books on self-help and palm reading in order to broaden your knowledge. You can never know too much. I've been reading palms all my life and I learn new things all the time. Use this information to help craft a better way of life for yourself before you rush out to save the world! Carefully examine your own hand as you read this book. After all, your hand is an extension of your soul. As you come to know your hand you will come to understand yourself better. Then you can help others achieve their own hidden potential.

I also want to take this opportunity to thank the many people who helped make this book possible: my good wife Elizabeth, who patiently tolerated the long hours I sat banging away at the word processor; master palmists Ron Martin and Sam Hawley, who provided invaluable input and insights during the early stages of planning this book and without whom I would probably never had the courage to begin such a difficult task; my good friend Richard Webster, who encouraged me to quit making excuses and start writing; E. Raymond Carlyle, my editor, who helped me keep my feet on the ground and pointed out areas where I wasn't making myself clear enough; and Fred Crouter, Ph.D., who made sure the psychological points were scientifically sound.

One final thing: as you read this book, don't forget to send out loving thoughts to the spirit of the mysterious Scandinavian whom fate brought into my family circle almost two hundred years ago. If it hadn't been for Sigurd/Siglinde, the secrets of runic palmistry would have been lost forever.

He who has seen and suffered much
And knows the way of the world,
He who has traveled can tell what spirit
Governs the people he meets.

THE POETIC EDDA

Part I

READING THE HAND

About astrology and palmistry: they are good because they make people vivid and full of possibilities. They are communism at its best. Everybody has a birthday and almost everybody has a palm . . . We would be a lot safer if the Government would take its money out of science and put it into astrology and the reading of palms.

KURT VONNEGUT, JR.

1

AN INTRODUCTION
TO PALMISTRY

*I'd trust a good palmist over a barrelful of
politicians any day . . .*

ALAIN "DOC" DELYLE

There's little wonder that palmistry has such a wide appeal.
Humans have always been fascinated with hands and what could
be learned by studying them. Palmistry goes back so many thousands of years nobody knows who the first palmists were. The oldest surviving document devoted to palmistry was found in India
and appears to be about 3,500 years old. However, we suspect that
the art is even older than this. After all, some of the earliest cave
paintings were of the artist's own hands!

Palmistry isn't strictly a psychic ability like clairvoyance or see-
ing auras. It's really a form of character analysis based on certain
features found in the hand. Anyone can learn to read palms after a
fashion, but it helps if you're naturally empathic and intuitive.
After studying a few thousand hands, the ability becomes ingrained

into the subconscious and you stop reading hands and begin to read people. The best palm readers go beyond the hand of the subject and into their soul. Think of the hand as the gateway into the personality.

The Visible Part of the Brain

The basic theory of palmistry teaches that the brain and the hand are closely connected. The hand is the visible agent of the brain—an extension of the mind—and through our hands we manipulate the world around us. Our hands reflect our moods and thoughts. When we are angry, we will express this emotion through the hands with clenched fists or a jabbing forefinger. When we're happy or depressed, we hold our hands differently. Over time, these habitual mannerisms and gestures of our unique personalities are recorded on our hands. This is a concept so natural that even most skeptics will agree there must be something to it.

Which Hand to Read?

You will hear this question almost every time you begin a reading. To do a thorough job you should look at both hands. However for a quick reading you will want to see the dominant hand. On a right-handed person, the left hand is considered the hand of *past influences* and the right hand represents *present circumstances*.

When we are born, both hands are pretty much the same. As we mature, the dominant hand changes faster, acting as the agent of our thoughts and desires. We write, eat, defend ourselves, and caress our loved ones with this hand. Consequently, as we react to the world, the dominant hand records these changes. The passive hand evolves too, but at a much slower rate. This is why palmists say the right hand represents the present and the left hand reveals the past. Some schools consider the left hand the repository of past-life information and karmic issues, but this concept is beyond the scope of this book.

Different Strokes for Different Folks

Different types of people have different types of hands. Obviously there is going to be a difference between the hand of an artist and the hand of a teamster. However, the differences in our hands can be even subtler. It's possible to make a distinction between the hand of a "thinker" and that of a "feeler." The hand of a natural-born counselor will show both thinking and feeling traits, while the hand of a scientist will show the qualities of logic and concentration.

The techniques of palmistry are meant to give you an overall picture of the person for whom you are reading. Everyone is unique, and a good palmist must tailor the information to match the person. It's important to make your reading fit your client, not the other way around. Never generalize!

Nothing Is Insignificant

In palmistry, every detail of the hand has meaning. We consider the relationships between the fingers, the lines on the hands, the skin ridge patterns (dermatoglyphics—an art in itself), the temperature and ruddiness of the skin, and even the hair pattern and skin texture. Some palmists believe that there are no such things as accidents and even scars and injuries to the hand may have special meanings.

Science has recently taken a serious look into hand analysis and a number of medical conditions can be detected through the study of the hands and nails. I personally do not diagnose medical conditions and neither should you unless you happen to have medical training.

Practice, Practice, Practice!

If you aspire to exercise your skills on others, be sure to take your time and learn your craft well. Practice on yourself first before starting on your friends' hands. Be careful and considerate. Do not trespass into areas where you're not qualified. Remember that it is not a reader's business to give financial, legal, or medical advice. We're concerned with spiritual and psychological matters and to step beyond these boundaries is illegal and unethical. Make the commitment from the outset to be a good and ethical reader, and always remember to be tactful.

As in any form of psychic reading or divination, you must approach the subject with serious intent. Do not perform palmistry as a psychic magick trick or do it because you like being the "class mystic." Whenever you're giving a reading you are literally holding that person's life in your hands. You have the potential to do great good—but also great harm. Never forget this.

How to Begin

A logical procedure is important. In runic palmistry, all aspects of the hand will be considered and it's easy for even an experienced reader to get lost. Therefore, it's important to have a logical sequence to follow or you'll probably overlook something important.

The first thing I suggest you notice is the shape of the hand. This provides a clue to the person's instinctive reactions to life. For example, round hands tend to be feelers and creators; square hands are thinkers and planners, and so on. Don't worry about trying to remember this right now. I'll go into more detail in chapter 3.

Go from General to Specific Details

After determining the shape of the hand, you're ready to move on to the fingers. Fingers reveal how people manipulate the world around them. Each finger has a different meaning, which we'll examine in more detail in chapters 4 and 5.

Next you will begin to interpret the branches and mounts in the hands. This will allow you to fine-tune the reading to razor-point accuracy. We'll look at this closely in chapters 6 and 7.

And finally, you'll locate the palm runes and interpret them. This exciting procedure will be touched on in the second half of this book, along with two simple methods of runecasts.

You are about to embark on a wonderful journey of self-discovery. I hope you'll find the trip as fascinating as I have. Have fun!

> *Cattle die, kindred die*
> *Every man is mortal.*
> *But the good name never perishes*
> *Of one who has done well.*
>
> THE POETIC EDDA

2

A Brief History of the Vikings

A furore normannorum libera nos domine
Skona oss herre från nordmännens raseri.

Oh Lord, save us from the rage of the Nordic people.

NINTH-CENTURY FRENCH PRAYER

The Norse religion was practiced by the Vikings, who hailed from ancient Iceland, Sweden, Norway, and Denmark. We know very little about the Viking's culture. What information we have survived mainly though scraps of legend and folklore. When Christianity swept across the northern countries during the Middle Ages, most of the Norse tradition was eradicated. The Catholic Church despised the Pagan religion, possibly due in part to the fact that between A.D. 700 until A.D. 1300 the Vikings made periodic raids on European monasteries. Despite these efforts, the old religion hung on for quite some time as it was conveyed orally from generation to generation. Amulets from the Middle Ages have been found in Iceland that depict both Thor's hammer and the Christian cross side by side.

Considering their primitive technology, the achievements of the Vikings seem miraculous. Fearless sailors and explorers, the Vikings were the first Europeans to pass the winter in Labrador and Newfoundland. They settled colonies in America long before anyone else. They populated the Hebrides, Greenland, Iceland, the Faroe Islands, Orkney, the Shetland Islands, and the Isle of Man. They settled in Ireland, Britain, Jerusalem, and Alexandria. They sired a Normandy dynasty in France that ruled well into the Middle Ages. Over nine hundred English words and over six hundred village names in England come from the Vikings. These people got around!

As master traders, the Vikings built merchant towns in Sweden, Denmark, and Norway. In Russia, they built trade stations along the rivers that stretched from the Black Sea to the Caspian Sea. Today, millions of Russian people have the names Oleg, Olga, and Igor from the names of the Viking gods Helge, Helga, and Ingvar. They conquered London, besieged Lisbon, burned Santiago, assaulted Seville, attacked Mallorca, terrorized Paris, and razed numerous German cities.

Most of what we know of Norse mythology comes from two surviving poems, the *Poetic Edda* (author unknown) and the *Prose Edda*. The *Prose Edda* is attributed to the Icelandic author Snorri Sturluson, who wrote most of his works between A.D. 1223–1235. While most scholars agree the *Poetic Edda* is the most important work, Snorri provides information not contained in the older saga. The oldest copy of the *Poetic Edda* dates around the beginning of the twelfth century, but the poems are purely Pagan and according to scholars are very, very old.

The Norse Creation Legend

According to the *Poetic Edda,* in the beginning was *Ginunga-gap* (geh-NUN-ga-gahp), the great Void. To the north of the Void was *Niflheim* (NIV-el-hame), the icy land of the dead. To the south was *Muspelheim* (MUZ-pel-hame), the land of fire. The interaction of ice and fire created the first life forms on the planet, the giant *Ymir* (EE-mir), and the ice maidens. This story bears remarkable similarities to scientists' theories that life first formed on Earth as volcanic heat interacted with the polar seas.

Created along with Ymir was the cow *Audumla* (*ow-DUM-lah*). Audumla formed the first god *Buri* (*BYU-ree*) by licking ice. In this unusual manner the first people were introduced into the universe.

According to the *Edda,* the god *Odin* (*OH-din* or *OO-dan*) and his two brothers killed Ymir and fashioned the world from his carcass. They turned his body into *Midgard,* where humans would live. The gods lived in *Asgard,* separated from Midgard by a rainbow bridge (*Bifrost*). This bridge was guarded by the giant *Heimdall,* who never slept and could see in the dark. The enormous ash tree *Yggdrasil* (*IG-dra-sil*) supported the entire universe. Its roots grew through all the worlds and nourished all life.

Races other than gods, humans, and giants also lived in the Norse world. Elves, dwarves, dragons, mermaids, frost giants, and a seemingly endless list of monsters inhabited their various domains.

This complicated picture had a dark side. The Norse universe had been destined for destruction from the moment of its creation. Even the gods knew that nothing could last forever. The sibyl in the *Poetic Edda* sings:

> *The Gods are doomed and the end is death.*
> *Earth sinks into the sea, the sun turns black.*
> *Cast from Heaven, the hot stars fall from the sky.*
> *Fumes reek, fire leaps high about Heaven*
> *The sky itself burns.*

Unlike the Greek gods who were immortal, the Norse gods knew that their reign was destined to end. The *Norns* (goddesses of fate) decreed that one day the forces of evil would assault Asgard and destroy the gods and all their works. The Norse gods lived with the realization that one day they would die. They knew exactly when, the day, and the hour. Even the world tree Yggdrasil would be destroyed, gnawed apart by serpents that lived among its roots.

Nor were humans to be spared this fate. When a brave Viking died, his soul was conveyed to *Valhalla* by Odin's handmaidens, the *Valkyries.* There he feasted and fought all day. At night he was restored and made ready to fight again the next day. This was to prepare him for *Ragnarok,* the great final battle the gods and their brave warriors were destined to lose.

The Viking idea of the afterlife was decidedly different from that of any other religion. We're accustomed to thinking of heaven as an eternal paradise where we live in ecstasy forever. We have an innate belief that good will always triumph over evil. This was not so with the Vikings. They knew that the world of gods and men would be destroyed at Ragnarok, but were bravely determined to go down fighting. This gloomy eventuality didn't matter to the Viking. The important thing was to fight and die heroically.

There is an old Norse tale about a Viking who was being killed by his enemies. He laughed at them while they cut the heart from his living body. He knew that all they could do was kill him—which meant very little, as long as he died bravely. The worst fate was called a *straw death,* meaning to die on the straw bed, or to die in one's sleep.

This worldview may strike us as fatalistic, but to the Viking this was just the way things were. Not all was bleak though. The *Edda* promised that after Ragnarok a new, brighter world would arise from the ashes of the old:

> *In wond'rous beauty, the dwellings roofed with gold.*
> *The fields unsowed bear ripe fruit in happiness forevermore.*

Perhaps this code of unflagging heroism is why a relatively small population of Vikings (around 800,000) was able to conquer most of the world. Due to their restless explorations and worldwide colonization, you can probably find a Viking among your ancestors no matter what your racial background.

The Vikings were our parents and grandparents. Their traditions and teachings are our heritage, passed down through time. We'll learn more about these teachings as we study the art of runic palmistry.

An Overview of the Principal Norse Deities

In most Western countries the archetypes used in palmistry are derived from Greco-Roman mythology and incorporate such familiar gods as Jupiter, Apollo, Mercury, and so on. This practice dates from a time when European palmists attempted to combine palmistry and astrology to create an overall picture of mystical influences. The Greek archetypes also function as memory aids, helping us link various aspects of the hand with specific psychological traits. It's a very useful tool.

The main difference I noticed in my family's technique was that the various parts of the hand were named after Norse gods such as *Odin, Thor,* and *Freya.* As you will see, the Norse gods were very different from their Greek counterparts, and these idiosyncrasies provide added dimensions to the interpretations. For your information, here are some of the most important Norse deities:

Aegir (*EE-jir*): His name is similar to the Norse word for water. Aegir is the personification of the ocean. Reknowned for his hospitality, the cups in Aegir's hall were always full, magically refilling on command. His aspects are located in the angle between the thumb and forefinger. Keywords: hospitality, service, tolerance.

Bragi (*BRAH-gee*): The Norse god of poetry. Bragi was so eloquent it was said he had runes cut on his tongue. His aspects are found in the third finger. Keywords: creativity, artistic ability, harmony.

Eir (*yeer*): Goddess of healing who taught the healing arts to women in ancient Scandinavia. Her aspects are found on the hands of natural healers. Keywords: healing, empathy, therapeutic skills.

Erda (*AIR-da*): Germanic aspect of Jorda, the Norse earth goddess. Related to the earth hand in palmistry. Keywords: practical, simple, down-to-earth.

Forseti (*for-SET-ee*): God of justice. His name means "presiding one." It was said he was "the god that stills all strife." His aspects are found on the middle joint of some thumbs. Keywords: tact, mediation, diplomacy.

Frey (*fray*): God of weather. Related to the air hand in palmistry. Keywords: unpredictable, independent, attracting attention.

Freya (*FRAY-ah*): Goddess of love, fertility, war, and wealth. Friday is named after her. One of the major branches of the palm reveals her aspects. Keywords: passion, sexuality, energy.

Heimdall (*HAME-doll*): Watches the rainbow bridge Bifrost for the coming of enemies. He never sleeps, can see in the dark, and can hear sheep's wool growing. Related to the water hand in palmistry. Keywords: alertness, vigilance.

Hel (*hel*): Daughter of Loki, Hel is the goddess of the underworld. Her domain is *Elvidnir*, which means "misery." She was described as half living human and half corpse. Hel's aspects are found in a mount near the wrist on the heel side of the hand. Keywords: hidden fears, phobias, anxieties, negative influences.

Hoenir (*HAY-ner*): He gave intelligence to the first humans. His aspects are found in the second finger. Keywords: teacher, mentor, instructor.

Idun (*EE-doon*): Goddess who is the keeper of the apples that keep the gods eternally young. Goddess of youth, her name means "the rejuvenating one." Her aspect is found in a mount at the base of the thumb. Keywords: childlike self-expression, youthfulness.

Jorda (*YER-da*): Norse aspect of the earth goddess Erda. Her aspects are found on the mount behind the thumb. Keywords: love of nature, pioneer, love of freedom.

Lofn (*LOW-fin*): Goddess concerned with sparking passionate love. She had permission from Odin and *Frigg*, Odin's wife, to do so even for those who were forbidden to marry. Her aspects are located in a triangular area found in some hands. Keywords: sexual indiscretion, infatuations.

Loge (*LOW-gi*): Loge is wildfire, and he appears in the story "Thor and Loki Among the Giants" which is found later in this book. Keywords: intense, curious, passionate.

Loki (*LOW-kee*): A giant, the personification of mischief, a trickster, and very cunning. His aspects are seen in the little finger. Keywords: wit, communication, manipulation, salesmanship.

Mimir (*MEE-mir*): A wise being—in some myths a god and in others a giant. Odin bartered one of his eyes for a drink from Mimir's well, which was said to give infinite wisdom. One of the branches of the palm reveals his aspects. Keywords: logic, wisdom, intelligence, the mind.

Nanna (*NAN-ah*): Goddess of the moon. Keywords: empathy, intuition, insight.

Odin (*OH-din* or *OO-dan*): Chief of the gods. Known as "the All-Father" and "the Wanderer." His aspects are found in the forefinger. Keywords: ego, control, knowledge.

Saga (*SAH-ga*): Goddess of history. Her aspects are found in the middle joint of the thumb. Keywords: logic, tradition, mental abilities.

Sif (*sif*): Goddess of crops and fertility. Married to Thor. Her aspects are found in the pad of the thumb and in one of the major branches of the palm. Keywords: fertility, sexual passion, sensuality.

Thor (*thor*): The son of Odin, Thor was the god of thunder. Not exactly a master of tact, he smashed enemies with his mighty hammer *Mjollnir* (*MYOL-nir*). His aspects are found in the tip of the thumb. Keywords: willpower, stubbornness, independence.

Tyr (*tur*): God of war. Tuesday is named for Tyr. Keywords: aggression, bravery, underhandedness.

Now that you know a little bit about Norse mythology, we can begin reading palms the runic way. We'll be examining these Norse gods in greater detail throughout the book. You may want to come back to this section to refresh your memory as you learn the various aspects of runic palmistry.

Once he has won wealth enough
One should not crave more.
What he saves for friends
May be stolen by enemies.

THE WORDS OF THE HIGH ONE

3

THE FOUR ELEMENTS OF THE HAND

In all countries, in all civilizations, the study of the hand
has always been associated with the study of Life itself.

COUNT LOUIS HAMON (CHEIRO),
YOU AND YOUR HAND

Learning to recognize the different shapes of the hand can be challenging. Some palmistry books list as many as thirty-six different hand types! I know from experience that this can be intimidating when you're first starting to learn palmistry. Luckily, it's not as difficult as it first appears. Nor should this important step be neglected. The shape of the hand is our first glimpse into a person's character and can tell us a great deal. For example, square hands generally belong to thinkers while round hands are more likely to belong to feelers. Think of the shape of a hand as a clue to a person's instinctive reaction to the world, or how one reacts on the subconscious level to an environment. This will become clearer as we examine the four elemental hand types.

The Four Elemental Types

To keep it as simple as possible, we'll draw upon time-tested concepts and divide hands into four types named after the elements earth, air, fire, and water. The famous palmist Fred Gettings was fond of this classification system and you'll find it extremely useful in runic palmistry. The four elements were also used by my grandmother and Aunt Eliza, and you can't get any higher recommendation than that!

One caution: In practice you will find that most people will not have a pure hand type, but instead their hands will combine elements from two or more types. It helps if you mentally subdivide the hand into two parts: the fingers and the palm. Palms are either round or square, and fingers are either long or short. This is a spectacular oversimplification, but it works well enough in the beginning. Over time you will refine your classification system and your readings will become more accurate. Working from photocopies will be a great help.

Although learning to identify the shapes of the hands is a bit tricky, you'll develop the knack fairly quickly with practice. The following are the four elemental hand types.

Erda—The Earth Hand

The *Erda hand* is the easiest of the four types to recognize. The two qualities to look for are a square palm and short fingers (Figure 3.1). Usually the Erda hand contains very few lines or branches, which reflects the person's preference for simplicity. If the fingers are rounded at the tips, the person may be a bit impatient. Square tips suggest more tolerance. The subject possessing an earth hand will be practical, down-to-earth (naturally), reliable, predictable, emotionally stable, and often conservative. The line patterns of these hands are usually very simple, which reflect the person's simple and direct approach to life.

The earth hand denotes people who are fond of tradition. Their motto is "If it isn't broke, don't fix it." They possess a strong work ethic, are punctual, and tend to provide for the future. They neither lead nor follow, preferring instead

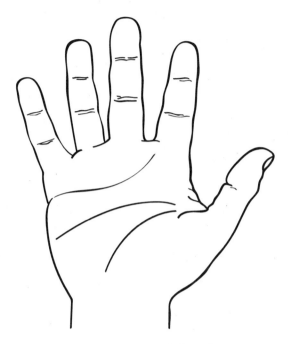

FIGURE 3.1—Erda hand

to do things their own way in their own time. This hand type is often found on architects, craftspeople, and designers. Earth people are usually fond of plants and animals.

Think of the earth when you see this hand. Mountains and trees tend to be very stable and move slowly. The earth is fertile, so this hand reveals an active interest in sex. Although the earth person usually isn't the most passionate romantic, they are nurturing and supportive. For the Erda, relationships do not burn like fire, nor do they flow like water, but are sources of security and stability. Because of this love of security, fire and water people tend to think earth people are boring.

Loge—The Fire Hand

Fire hands have short fingers which denote impatience, with a long palm which indicates their vast reserves of emotional energy (Figure 3.2). The Loge hand is

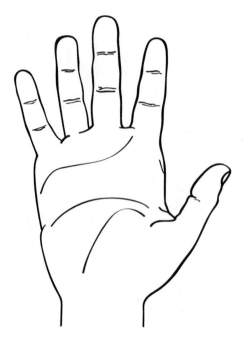

FIGURE 3.2—Loge hand

usually hot to the touch. People with this hand type are passionate and intense. They love change and variety, and become easily bored with tedious work. They hate restrictions, limitations, or falling into a rut.

Loge was the god of fire and he consumed everything in his path. Consequently, fire people possess strong desires, appetites, and ambition. Great starters, they seldom finish their projects. They become inflamed with an idea but lack the patience to see it through. They become bored if something takes too long to finish and rush off to begin a new project! Fire and earth work well together; the Loge starts the project and turns it over to the Erda who finishes it.

Fire is ambitious, and if the fire element is too strong it can make a person greedy and power-hungry. Loges have to be reminded how their actions affect others. Otherwise their ambition can cause them to run over others on the way to their goal. A fire hand with a tempering element of earth or water is ideal.

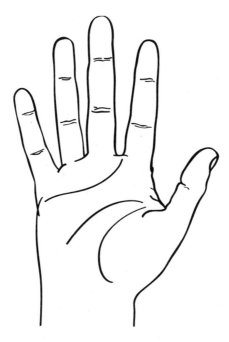

FIGURE 3.3—Frey hand

Fire can only burn so long. Addicted to intense action, Loges will frequently crash after a period of strenuous activity. But they will have accomplished a great deal in a short amount of time.

Frey—The Air Hand

Recognizable by its square palm and long fingers (Figure 3.3), the *air hand* denotes people with quick, agile minds. The negative side of the air hand is that these people tend to deceive and manipulate. Freys are great self-motivators and work according to their own inner agenda. Frey was the god of weather, so his people go wherever the wind, or their fancy, blows them. They can be a bit flamboyant in their behavior and they don't always mean what they say!

As natural entertainers, Freys tend to enjoy attention and recognition. They thrive on mental challenges and work well under a deadline. Sometimes they seem to be addicted to stress and melodrama. Naturally explorative and curious, a Frey person will try anything at least once.

Versatile and multisided, it is as though Freys have several different people living in their head. I have a Frey hand, and my Aunt Eliza always said I was like "an engineer trapped inside the body of a psychologist!" I couldn't agree more.

Many actors sport a Frey hand. Freys are great at debate and often will argue either side of an issue just for the fun of it. They enjoy psychology and playing mind games with themselves as well as with others. Frey was responsible for the fruits of the earth, so people with his hand are very good at generating concepts, theories, and ideas (sowing the seeds), although they seldom find the time to act on all of them.

Heimdall—The Water Hand

A *water hand* will combine a long palm with many fine lines and long fingers (Figure 3.4). Water is the most volatile and unstable of the four elements. After all, earth is always earth, and fire is always fire, but water can be liquid, solid, or gaseous. It can be said that water can take on the states of the other three elements as well as its own. Therefore Heimdall people tend to be moody, and at times their external appearance is completely at odds with the internal reality. "You can't judge a book by its cover" is definitely true of water people. They are often plagued by mood swings and conflicting impulses as they shift from an earthlike (solid) state to airlike (gaseous) state. Also, the long fingers denote perfectionism and sensitivity to detail. Heimdall people can be difficult to please. Aunt Eliza calls them "choicy."

Because of the myriad tiny lines covering their surfaces, Heimdall hands tend to look old. Many times when I have given readings to people with Heimdall hands they have apologized for how old their hands look. I always remind them that the lines have nothing to do with age but with the intensity of their emotional expression. I show them a print of the hand of a fourteen-year-old Heimdall with the comment "If you were to judge her age from her hands, you

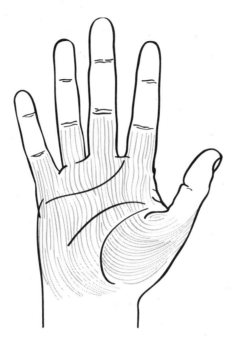

FIGURE 3.4—Heimdall hand

would think she was ninety!" Always try to find something nice to say about a Heimdall's hands as they tend to be self-conscious about their appearance.

It's difficult to read water people's moods from their faces as "still waters run deep." Ruled by Heimdall, the ever-vigilant guard of the Rainbow Bridge, they are watchers and observers. This holds especially true if the fingers are knobby. The god Heimdall's senses were said to be so acute he could hear grass growing. Heimdall people love to watch and observe others.

Water hands are restless and need a grounding influence or they will tend to scatter their energy all over the place. Heimdalls approach subjects indirectly and can talk for hours about nothing in particular. However, when grounded by a solid relationship, religious doctrine, or profession, they can be tremendously productive and creative. Because they love to approach a subject from oblique angles, Heimdalls have unique perspectives and their own way of doing things.

Heimdalls tend to be sensitive to criticism and often see rejection where none was intended. On the other hand, they can be quite intuitive, and their first impressions of people are often right on target.

Interpreting the Hand Types

Now that you know the four elemental hand types, you can start classifying the hands of anyone lucky enough to be within reach! As I pointed out earlier, you will find that most people exhibit a combination of two or more hand types. Typically you'll find that the fingers are of one type and the palm of another. The person, then, will be a blend of the two hand types. If someone has an Erda (earth) palm with Loge (fire) fingers, this person will be down-to-earth and practical but with a strong curiosity and a need for mental stimulation. Just remember that the palm represents the unconscious instincts, while the fingers represent how these instinctive needs are manifested in the real world.

Some Other Interesting Hand Types

As I mentioned earlier, many palmistry books list a bewildering array of different hand types. Here are a few of the most common ones to add to your collection.

The Conic Hand

A very beautiful type, the almond-shaped *conic hand* represents a refined, sensitive, and empathic person (Figure 3.5). A true conic hand should have a smooth curve, finely textured skin, and tapering fingertips. On a male it indicates a sympathetic, sensitive, and intuitive outlook—not your average macho type! If you want to see an outstanding example of this hand type, take a look at the *Mona Lisa*. Her hands are textbook conic.

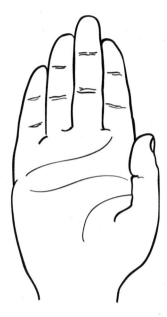

Figure 3.5—Conic hand

The Spatulate Hand

The *spatulate hand* is easy to spot because the palm looks like a spatula—wider at one end than the other (Figure 3.6). True spatulate hands will have splayed fingertips as well. Spatulate people have a lot of internal energy and are always on the go. They tend to be a bit nervous, fantasy-prone, and at times unrealistic. They make great actors because they are extremely good at make-believe. I call them "shape-shifters" and they usually agree.

The Philosopher's Hand

The *philosopher's hand* is a square hand with long, knobby fingers (Figure 3.7). Possessed of an unusually analytical mind, people with these hands can really put things under a microscope. For example, in an argument they can tell you exactly what's wrong with you, and what you need to do to fix it! They're truly excellent at looking below the surface of a thing and figuring out how it works.

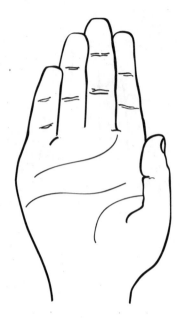

FIGURE 3.6—Spatulate hand

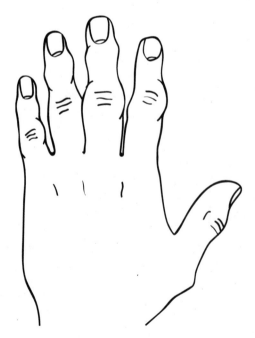

FIGURE 3.7—Philosopher's hand

Final Thoughts

Don't be discouraged if it takes you a while to catch on to the various hand types. It takes experience to quickly identify the elements of the hand, but it's a compelling study and you'll get better with practice. Master palmist Ron Martin suggests you work from photocopies of your friend's hands before subjecting live people to your scrutiny. Many palmistry texts feature the handprints of celebrities, which can also be a great learning tool. And in your early attempts at live reading, you can ask your volunteers to give you plenty of feedback. They'll set you straight!

A kind word need not cost much
The price of praise can be cheap.
With half a loaf and an empty cup
I found myself a friend.

THE WORDS OF THE HIGH ONE

4

THE FINGERS

Let us be easy and impersonal, not forever fingering over our own souls, and the souls of our acquaintances, but trying to create a new life, a new common life, a new complete tree of life from the roots that are within us.

D. H. LAWRENCE

If the palm of the hand is a storage battery, then the fingers are the organs that project this energy into the world. The fingers represent our cognitive functions and include communication skills, self-image, moral sense, self-expression, and many other important characteristics that determine how we function in the world.

We already picked up a few interesting facts about the fingers in the previous chapter. For example, we've seen that people with short fingers tend to be impatient. They will hate sitting around all day, waiting for something to happen or for someone to make up their mind. When they get behind a slow-moving truck or a little old man counting out change in the grocery line, it's agony! On the other hand, they can appraise an unfamiliar situation very quickly and make the right decision guided by their instincts.

Long fingers do not necessarily indicate patience, but rather attention to detail. People with long, tapered fingers will be detail-sensitive to the point of perfectionism. If the fingers are long and crooked, they will be self-critical, turning that perfectionism against themselves. They will find fault with the tiniest flaw in their appearance or action, and no amount of reassurance will convince them otherwise.

Interesting as these little insights are, let me assure you that there's more to the fingers than just their length! Each finger is named after one of the Norse gods. Please familiarize yourself with Figure 4.1, which shows the god associated with each finger. We will discuss each of these fingers in detail. The thumb, which is a special case, will be discussed in a later chapter. You'll be amazed at how much you can learn about people from just a quick look at their fingers alone!

Odin—The Warrior

In palmistry the forefinger represents the ego, control issues, and self-image. For this reason we call it the *finger of Odin,* the chief of the gods. The finger is considered strong if it is longer than the third finger (Figure 4.2) or if it is especially thick. The finger of Odin represents how we want others to see us. It's important to remember that this is the external persona, not how we really are deep inside. Think of this public image as a mask worn when we deal with other people. There's often a huge discrepancy between self-image and public image. With a person with a strong Odin finger you can count on it.

Why the Ego?

Psychologically, the forefinger represents control and assertiveness. A strong Odin finger indicates a person's inclination toward leadership, independence, and self-reliance. Wearing a ring on the forefinger shows a subconscious desire to dominate. It's on this finger that caesars and popes wear their ring of authority. Odin was referred to as "the All-Father," so parents point the Odin finger at their children as they give them direction.

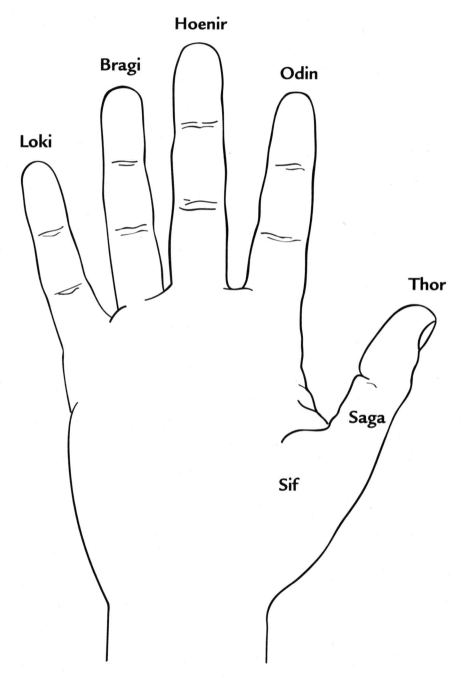

FIGURE 4.1—The Norse deities associated with each finger

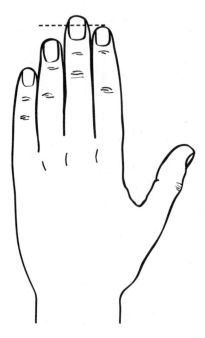

FIGURE 4.2—Long Odin finger

Odin, the leader of the Norse gods, had many aspects, including god of war, poetry, wisdom, and death. Therefore people with strong Odin tendencies will usually be involved in many projects, have numerous irons in the fire, and quite often play several social and professional roles simultaneously. They love travel, hate sitting still, and are restless. They're among the most responsible people in the world, and the most assertive.

Odin was an aggressive, warlike god, which is why we always interpret a forefinger pointed at us as an attack. We naturally become defensive when stabbed by "Odin's Spear."

Relative Length of Odin

A forefinger that is significantly longer than the third finger (Bragi) can denote a personality that is predominantly Odin-driven. When the finger is noticeably fuller, bigger, and more powerful, the Odin force is strong. Always keep in mind that appearances are very important to Odins. They're extremely proud, and to look at them you would think that they're always in control. On the outside they appear to be cool, confident, and aloof. On the inside, however, you'll usually find a different story. All that responsibility creates an internal nervousness that can lead to strong uncertainty much of the time. But they'll never show it. Odins are good at keeping a brave front in the face of disaster. They hate to admit that anything is wrong; to them this indicates weakness.

Imagine the responsibility of being the one who controls everything! When Odin people's lives get out of balance, they become uncannily calm on the surface. The worse the disaster, the more in control they seem. Think of a captain calmly going down with his sinking ship and you'll get the picture.

Use Caution

Before you accuse a long-forefingered person of being egocentric, be sure to consider all the other factors found in the hand. Emphasize the positive qualities before pointing out the negative. Remember to always be tactful. Odin people possess a great deal of pride and they don't take criticism very well.

Odin people are good at giving direction, but seldom take their own advice. Even less will they take advice from others. They are better at giving orders than obeying them, so don't try to tell them what they need to do. They'll simply tune you out.

I usually tell Odins, "You have a strong Odin finger, which means you like to feel in control of all aspects of your life. You're good at instructing people what to do, and you give good advice. Unfortunately, you do not always listen to your own good advice. You're a natural leader and you would be good with children. When you tell them to behave they will listen to you! Your pride is strong, and you hate to have to ask for help."

Interpreting the Odin and Bragi Balance

Traditionally the length of the forefinger is compared with that of the third finger. If it's considerably longer than the third finger (a nail's length or more), you're looking at a person in whom Odin is strong. If the forefinger is notice-ably shorter, Bragi probably rules the subject (more on Bragi later).

Emotional Balance

Ideally, the first and third fingers should be in balance. If the forefinger is equal in length to the third finger, it denotes an individual with a well-balanced ego. This person can be assertive without being aggressive. Such people make ideal managers because they can take the lead when necessary and put aside their ego long enough to be fair and even-handed. Their self-esteem is usually good and they tend to be growth-oriented. Self-improvement is important to them. They deal with challenges and new situations well, and when they are wrong they're the first to admit it. Bragis are peacemakers, diplomats, and delegators, and can draw upon this energy to temper the strength of the Odin forces.

The Seeker of Knowledge

Odin sacrificed himself for knowledge by hanging from the world tree Yggdrasil for nine days. In doing so, he learned the secrets of the runes. In *The Words of the High One*, Odin says:

> *Nine whole nights on a wind-rocked tree*
> *Wounded with sharp spear*
> *I was offered to Odin, myself to myself*
> *On that tree of which no man knows.*

The runes are symbols of great power. Odin passed his hard-won knowledge of the runes to humans, and we'll be taking a closer look at them in Part II. His thirst for knowledge was so great that he sacrificed one of his eyes to drink from Mimir's well, which was believed to bestow great knowledge. Because of this sac-rifice, Odin is typically depicted as having one eye. His one eye also represents single-mindedness, a trait often found in people ruled by Odin.

Odins crave knowledge more than food. It was said of the All-Father that he never ate with the other gods. Instead he gave his food to his pet wolves and thrived on the information his two crows, Memory and Thought, whis-pered in his ear. These two crows would fly all over the world to collect information for their master. Thus Odin people crave knowledge and power, and will do whatever is necessary (within reason, of course) to achieve it. On the plus side, they are always willing to share their knowledge with anyone who can benefit from it.

Relationships and the Odin Person

Relationships pose quite a challenge for the Odin person. As natural leaders, Odins love to control all the pathways of their lives, whether an issue is an important one or not. At times they're compelled to try to control the lives of others. Most Odins believe other people (especially loved ones) are incapable of taking care of themselves. Tact is an essential tool to use when dealing with your favorite Odin.

For the Odin person, surrender is very difficult and compromise presents a challenge. Two Odins under the same roof can resemble a wrestling match!

The Ego and Death

Odins resist change more than most. They'll stick with a terrible job or a bad relationship far longer than they should. They hate to give up!

Psychologically, the fear of change is synonymous with the fear of death. Both change and death represent forays into the unknown. Odins are uncomfortable with unknown territory; they like to be let in on the game plan. Accepting change is almost impossible for Odins.

One of my favorite Odins once told me: "For me to give control to anyone else means that I leave myself open to manipulation. I can't stand that. So I seek control of a situation even when the outcome is of little consequence to me." As a critical-care nurse who helped usher people to death's doorway with compassion and calm dignity, my friend thought, "For me, I guess, surrender of control is related to dying, and I'm not ready to die yet."

The Paradigm

Odin was the All-Father, the creator of reality, and ruler of the world. Therefore, it is not surprising that the ego is central to the Odin's mental map of the world. This map also influences how Odins respond to others. Odins are great at rationalizing discrepancies between reality and their own worldview. When threatened by new or alien concepts, Odins take things out of the world and put them in their head, where they can manipulate reality to suit themselves.

When introducing change into an Odin's life, do so in small, easily digestible bites. Since the Odin's favorite defense mechanism is intellectualization, you must give them time to fit each new piece of information into their worldview. They will embrace the change as long as they believe it was their idea to begin with!

Bragi—The Peacemaker

Skipping over the second finger for the moment, let's discuss what happens when the forefinger is shorter than the ring finger (Figure 4.3). In runic palmistry the ring finger is the *finger of Bragi*. When the third finger overshadows the influence of Odin, Bragi rules the person. Bragi was the Norse god of poetry and was so eloquent he was said to have runes cut on his tongue. For our purposes he represents the poetic, artistic, and literary creative forces. A true Bragi must have a well-developed third finger—long and straight and noticeably longer than the forefinger.

Self-Doubt and the Bragi

The Bragi personality with a short forefinger tends to have serious doubts about their own abilities. It's common for Bragi people to underestimate their own competency in their chosen field. Depending on the degree of disparity between the first and third finger, Bragis may have to overcome a measure of initial shyness before embarking into the unknown.

Bragis will avoid direct confrontation and prefer harmony in the home and workplace. But in spite of their peaceful nature, Bragis seem to find themselves in the middle of conflict much of the time, acting as interlocutors, peacemakers, or diplomats. In psychological terms they are *adjusters,* trying to bring harmony and balance to the conflicts that seem to always surround them.

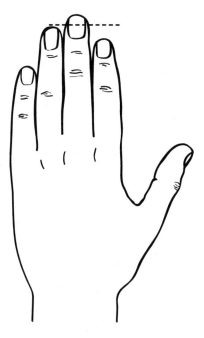

FIGURE 4.3—Long Bragi finger

When Bragis desire something strongly, they tend to go after it strategically. They prefer to use persuasion to achieve their ends, rather than strength of will as an Odin would.

The Undeveloped Bragi

When strong, Bragis can achieve great prominence in their creative field. But when the Bragi energy is blocked or underdeveloped, the person's potential will remain hidden.

Try this little game with yourself. Look at the fingers of your dominant hand. Consciously attempt to change the length of your forefinger, stretching it longer or compressing it shorter. You'll find you can make the forefinger longer or shorter with little effort. When a person withdraws emotionally, the musculature of the hand pulls back, causing the appearance of a short forefinger. When a person becomes more assertive, the forefinger seems to lengthen. There's nothing mystical in all this; it's well-known that the mind cannot experience anything without the body reflecting it physically.

The Odin/Bragi balance happens to be the ego's emotional barometer. Are you the family adjuster, the person who yields in the relationship, or the peace-maker? You are probably the passive Bragi with a short forefinger. If you are boisterous, funny, and extroverted and if you love being in the limelight, you are probably an assertive Bragi with the first and third fingers in balance.

Relationships and the Bragi Person

Bragis need a great deal of encouragement and support. They often blow small rejections out of proportion. Therefore it's essential for the Bragi to avoid hostile, critical people and to associate with friendly, happy ones. Bragis have refined tastes and tend to be sentimental, romantic, and idealistic. Consequently they will often fall in love with love, and can be a bit naïve in relationships.

The Bragi's favorite defense mechanism is what psychologists describe as passive/aggressive behavior. Bragis tend to sulk when they don't get their way. Due to their lack of assertiveness they will often shut down emotionally and refuse to discuss with anyone what's bothering them. During this time, no amount of persuasion will force Bragis into a discussion before they are ready. All one can do is be patient; eventually they will emerge from their shell.

The Artful Designer

Finally we will consider Bragi's role as the patron god of musicians, poets, artists, and actors. Prominent Bragi fingers generally indicate people who avoid conflict and who possess a high aesthetic standard. These people know the right place for everything. They are the artists, actors, and designers of the world. Bragis tend to be attracted to art, literature, drama, and music.

Bragis are very sensitive to their surroundings and can become unfocused in a troubled environment. Peace and quiet are dear to their souls.

It's often difficult to understand what motivates Bragis. Artists are often described as "other-directed," meaning that they are not motivated by money, social acceptance, or worldly success. Many people of polite society do not understand why artists do what they do.

Bragis will tell you there are few things more satisfying than producing a work of art, whether you get paid for it or not. Creativity is essential for Bragis' survival and contentment. To them, the creative urge is an expression of the desire for immortality. The artist's mind is the reflection of the mind of God the Creator that shapes beauty out of dust.

The Bragi's Delicate Ego

It may take years for Bragis to be completely confident and comfortable with themselves, but the journey tends to become easier the further they go. They must work hard to develop confidence and independence. Sadly, a great many Bragis never seem to arrive at their full potential. Self-doubt, lack of encouragement and support (which Bragis seem to need more than most), passivity, and the tendency to wait to be discovered rather than spearhead their own success keeps a lot of Bragis from recognizing their great artistic and cultural gifts. Many unsung geniuses are undeveloped Bragis.

However, under the proper conditions Bragis can blossom into their full potential and make significant creative contributions to the world. It takes time. I've found that most strong Bragis are late bloomers; they come into their full awareness sometime during their late thirties and early forties.

Hoenir—The Philosopher

The second finger is the *finger of Hoenir*. Hoenir was a brother of Odin who, along with the third brother Lodur, helped create the world. It seems that Odin, Hoenir, and Lodur were walking on a beach when they came upon two trees, *Ash* and *Embla*. The three brothers decided to free these trees from the earth, and from them they fashioned the first humans. Each brother endowed the two humans with a special gift. The *Poetic Edda* says of the first men:

> *Breath they had not, nor blood nor senses*
> *Nor language possessed, nor life-hue;*

Odin gave them breath, Hoenir senses,
Blood and life-hue Lodur gave.

Thus Hoenir gave humans common sense and the ability to determine right from wrong.

Runic palmistry links Hoenir's finger to moral issues, self-discovery, and emotional stability. Wearing a ring on the middle finger can indicate a subconscious desire for isolation. Not surprisingly, a lot of people wear rings from ex-lovers on this finger.

Traditionally, a long, straight Hoenir finger indicates a person who is exceptionally moral and disciplined and concerned with issues of right and wrong. It is not surprising to see strong Hoenirs on the hands of judges and policemen.

Through metaphysical logic, it was formerly believed that a crooked middle finger implied a lack of morality. However, modern palmists associate this trait with an imbalanced moral sense. The direction of the crookedness reveals how the person's moral sense was affected by their upbringing.

The Pessimist

If the second finger leans toward Odin (the forefinger) (Figure 4.4), it will be dominated by authoritarian energy, causing the person to have a gloomy outlook about their future. These people will constantly experience doubt about their chances of success in a new undertaking. Sometimes it makes them so unsure of themselves that they will plan a new project forever and never allow it to leave the drawing board. In extreme cases, these people fear failure so much they hardly ever attempt anything even slightly risky. Always preferring to walk on safe ground, they seldom initiate any new or exploratory ideas.

Depression

Depression can be spotted by a long second finger that curves noticeably toward Bragi (the ring finger) (Figure 4.5). When you see this, you can rest assured these subjects are their own worst critics. They can be mercilessly hard on themselves. When someone attempts to praise them for their work, they

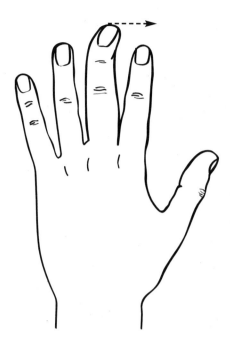

FIGURE 4.4—Hoenir leaning toward Odin

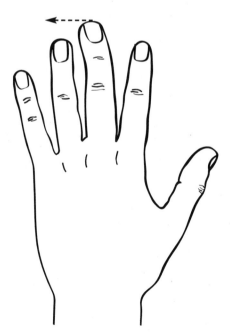

Figure 4.5—Hoenir leaning toward Bragi

reply, "No, no—you're too kind. I did a bad job. I didn't cross all the *t*'s or dot all the *i*'s." Nothing they do is ever good enough for them.

Possibly more attention has been focused on depression in the last ten years than on any other human mental condition. Affecting the body, mind, and spirit, clinical depression has been linked to the production of the neurotransmitter serotonin. Since mind, body, and spirit influence each other, successful treatment of depression must address all three of these aspects. Medication alone can only go so far. The mind and the spirit must be healed also.

This is where palm readers can provide their greatest contributions to the client. Depressive individuals have extraordinary abilities, which we will examine more closely in a moment. Their problems arise from an inability to freely express these unique abilities in the society that surrounds them.

Think of depressive people as the antennae of society, mentally in touch with everything that goes on around them. Psychologists report that depressed people are strongly affected by their environment. Even as newborns they react more energetically to movement and sound. Adult depressive people react to the environment and the changes of season. Depressive people are able to read emotional cues that many of us miss. They can sense when something is wrong or out of sync. In psychic circles, such people are known as *sensitives*.

In tribal days, sensitives acted as shamans and lay psychologists who helped ease conflicts and healed the troubled spirit. It was very desirable for the tribal community to have certain people who were sensitive and intuitive and who knew when danger or disaster was near. Their peers held them in high esteem.

This is not as true today as it used to be. In our technological society there is little place for such people. Sensitivity is discouraged. Aren't we told as children that "Sticks and stones will break your bones, but words will never hurt you"? But words do hurt, as do looks, gestures, and rejection. Sensitives are urged to invalidate their own feelings, suppress their unique gift, and see their greatest positive asset as a handicap. Is it any wonder that they experience feelings of despair and isolation?

This is not a minor problem. The result of untreated depression is quite often suicide. This is not surprising; without nurturing, any organism will perish. We see it through the study of fossil records, but more importantly, we see it immediately around us in society.

Depressive people are the repository of a society's spirituality. It is the work of sensitives to find an acceptable outlet for their gift. This can be a lonely task, involving a great amount of introspection and anxiety. In *The Road Less Traveled*, M. Scott Peck calls episodes of depression "spiritual crises." Depressed people are searching for their soul, and to be cured they must find it.

On the bright side, once these people pass through the chill waters of depression they will experience a wonderful change of perspective. The empathic response to pain becomes a bit mellower. Depression survivors are wonderfully sympathetic with an intuitive understanding of pain. A friend who suffered from depression and alcoholism once said, "After surviving depression and addiction, I know pain. You could drive my testicles through a tree stump with a twenty-pound sledgehammer and I would laugh at you—'You think that hurt?'" (Some of my friends tend to be a little melodramatic.)

The pharmacological treatment of depression has shown wonderful results, but the work remains for sensitives (as it does for each of us) to determine how they can best serve society. Depression lifts when people feel cherished and useful. Once a person finds a satisfying life path, the burden of depression becomes easier to bear.

Hoenir taught human beings to make full use of the gifts the gods gave them. Sadly, we've lost sight of this simple, but important, primal lesson.

Hoenir the Philosopher

There are, of course, other traits associated with Hoenir. Since this is the finger governing moral issues, it represents the part of us that questions the differences between right and wrong. This is an extremely important component of a well-balanced personality. In *The Words of the High One*, Odin reminds us, "Better equipment than good sense a traveler cannot carry."

Children learn morality from the actions of adults. This process can be enigmatic and inconsistent. Some adults say it's okay to play in mud puddles while others forbid it. It's all right to dig in the yard, but not in the flower bed!

Consider the following exchange: "Mommy, you have a phone call." "Tell them I'm not here." "But that's a lie!" "Just tell them, would you? It's okay." Over time the child learns these lessons well. In an attempt to undo the damage, the parent admonishes, "Don't do as I do. Do as I say!" Right. Did this work on you?

There's little wonder that most of us grow up not knowing exactly what to do with ourselves. We're constantly weighing the consequences of our actions and wondering if we're truly doing the right thing.

Negotiable Wrongs

Moral issues become even more confusing to a person who was raised in a dysfunctional home. In such homes, right and wrong are frequently negotiable. Some things are wrong some of the time, but not always.

> "Do not steal—unless it's from a company, the government, or from someone else who can afford it."

> "Do not lie—unless it keeps you out of trouble or helps you evade responsibility."

> "Violence solves nothing—unless your drunken father decides to beat up everyone in the family."

The finger of Hoenir helps us figure out how we adapted to these moral tugs-of-war. When the finger leans noticeably toward Odin, these people are probably products of this type of moral ambiguity. They will probably look to others for guidance. Each new situation becomes a crisis as they have to figure out the appropriate behavior. There are no certain answers for these people, no black-and-white rules exist. They tend to do whatever they're told by the nearest figure of authority. Hoenir leaning toward Bragi denotes a person whose highest law is compassion.

Amorality

If Hoenir is small, underdeveloped, or covered with crosshatches, the person may be amoral. Amorality is defined as the inability to determine right from wrong. Amorality is self-serving. The actions of amoral people are designed to satisfy their own needs with no concern for the feelings of others. They see the entire world as being in existence to serve them, and seldom do they suffer from remorse or self-doubt. Hopefully you won't see this very often.

The Dogmatic Do-Gooder

At the other end of the spectrum are people who were raised in an authoritarian home with strong moral lessons. Programmed at an early age with an inflexible moral code, these people tend to see issues of good and evil in black-and-white terms. Often they will adopt a religious or political philosophy that eliminates all the guesswork from their moral decisions. They can be quite ruthless within the boundaries of their self-imposed code of ethics.

The key to identifying this condition are large, rigid, and inflexible middle fingers that represent the unyielding nature of these people's moral stance. Gently bend the finger backward to test for resistance. If you have trouble bending the finger, it is considered inflexible. The problem with this end of the moral spectrum is that once this type becomes dogmatic about an issue, they stop thinking about it. No new ideas are allowed into the moral fortress and the other person's point of view becomes immaterial; learning stops. The word here is *bullheaded*.

When you encounter a rigid Hoenir, you might suggest that the person learn to relax a little—but the odds are against them listening to you. My favorite aunt says they could benefit from a swift kick in the behind to loosen them up!

Flexible Hoenir

Again, balance is important. Palmists learn to look for a firm, straight, and *flexible* Hoenir finger. Well-balanced Hoenirs have a basic moral compass that keeps them out of trouble most of the time. They will be open and receptive to new ideas and will often rethink and test their beliefs as new concepts are learned. These flexible people make wonderful parents as they encourage their children to think for themselves.

Hoenir the Teacher

A natural teacher is spotted when all three phalanges (sections) of the middle finger are of equal length. Avoiding extremes, they will find the middle path the most productive. When examining the morality of a certain action, these naturally inquisitive individuals will want to try everything out for themselves. They will constantly question and reexamine every aspect of their belief system.

This holds especially true with religious faith. These natural teachers believe that an unexamined faith is not a very strong one. A person with a well-balanced Hoenir will continue asking questions and learning about the world until the day they die, and they will delight in sharing their observations with others.

What Is Morality?

After all this discussion about the ins and outs of morality, we haven't really made a clear definition of what it is we're talking about. What constitutes moral behavior?

Morality isn't ethics, which is a code of behavior proper to a specific situation, nor is it duty, which is something that you are expected to do. In fact, sometimes duty, ethics, and morality will be at odds with one another. In a nutshell, morality is any action inspired by compassion. We can make it much more difficult than this (and indeed we do, which is why we have so much trouble with this simple concept), but in reality a compassionate person automatically does the right thing.

Compassion arises from the heart, not the head, and whenever people act out of compassion, they are expressing their capacity for love. Compassion makes us aware that the separation between "you" and "I" is an illusion; the fact is, anything you do to me you're also doing to yourself. It's as simple as that. No long list of rules to follow—just listen to your heart. If you'd like a second opinion, a great teacher once said, "Do unto others what you would have them do unto you," and "Love your neighbor as you would yourself." These are excellent rules to live by. It can't get much easier than this, can it?

Loki—The Mischief-Maker

The little finger of the hand belongs to Loki, the patron of salespeople, magicians, thieves, gypsies, storytellers, and essentially everyone who lives by their wits.

The Loki energy is strong when the little finger stands out from the hand away from the rest of the fingers (Figure 4.6). This represents Loki people's desire to stand apart from the crowd. They will thrive on independence. After all, people living by their wits would have a tendency to resist authority. Traditionally, wearing a ring on the pinky finger amplifies this sense of independence. Lokis would rather ask forgiveness than ask permission.

Communication skills are governed by Loki. A strong Loki finger gives a good sense of communication, charisma, and the ability to "sling it!" A talented salesman who could use his skills for good or bad, Loki acted as the

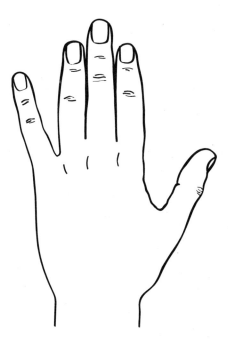

FIGURE 4.6—Independent Loki

gods' negotiator. But he double-crossed his employers whenever he felt it would serve his own best interests.

This is not to say that all Lokis are opportunists—most are not. Some of the most highly motivated and happy people in the world are Lokis. They take pride in making their living with their wits. Unfortunately, there is also a lot of stress involved, but Lokis seem able to handle it.

When the little finger curves in toward Bragi, it borrows some of the humanitarian instinct of that finger and creates the urge to use the Loki abilities to help others. Often Lokis will motivate by example, becoming excellent role models.

Independent Lokis relish their freedom. The gods punished Loki for his double-dealings by chaining him to a rock. Therefore, Lokis hate restrictions, limitations, or confinement. Even when Lokis work for a company, they are at their best if the boss just leaves them alone to run as they see best.

Relationships and Loki

Since Lokis require total autonomy, attempts to restrict or change them will only drive them away. Lokis thrive best in relationships that are open, free, and nonpossessive. Lokis value their privacy and are protective of their personal space, so do not crowd them or try to pry too deeply into their personal affairs. On the other hand, Lokis are creative lovers who will try anything if it sounds like fun. Just don't try to own them—they will simply disappear!

Lokis are mischievous and often have a strange sense of humor. They can be sarcastic, and will say or do bizarre things just to cause a reaction. Strong Lokis love to shock people.

Lokis enjoy being the center of attention and are often quite dramatic and entertaining. They can charm the pants off of anyone and sell the stripe off a skunk. Resourceful, they always land on their feet and always seem to have many schemes to get rich or to beat the odds. At times they can be a bit manipulative.

Loki's daughter was Hel, the queen of the underworld, born from his union with an evil giantess. Therefore, Lokis are often attracted to dangerous relationships and to people with a lot of problems. Lokis are fascinated by the human mind and often explore hypnosis, clairvoyance, and dream interpretation. They often have dark mood swings, during which their thinking becomes morbid and self-destructive. Usually these moods quickly pass and they're off again, planning their next scheme.

Since Lokis require lots of support and encouragement, the best possible mate for one would be a "cheerleader." But remember: That long little finger was just made for wrapping people around!

Lokis are born salespeople who flourish best when they are self-employed. They prefer to decide for themselves how much money they will make and how many hours they work. This element of control is the sweet appeal for independent Lokis, which more than compensates for the stress of becoming their own boss.

The Dependent Loki

When the little finger hugs very close to the third (Bragi) finger, or perhaps even overlaps it (Figure 4.7), it can indicate a dependent personality. This

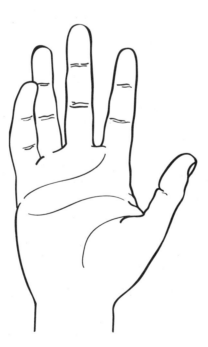

FIGURE 4.7—Dependent Loki

person will crave love and affection, and will often go to great efforts to obtain it. In moderation it makes the person clingy and outwardly shy. In extreme cases the individual will totally rely upon another person for economic and emotional support.

To illustrate this last point, I can do no better than to share with you an experience I had during a psychic fair several years ago, which involved the most frightening example of dependency I have ever encountered. At this particular psychic festival, I read for two sisters. The older sister was a little unsettling. She had pale green eyes and watched me attentively, a little (I imagined) like a wary cat watching for a chance to get the family canary. Her hand was strongly independent. I was glad when the reading was finished. Something about her was disturbing, although I couldn't quite put my finger on it.

A few minutes later her sister sat down for a reading. I noticed her extremely dependent Loki and planned to address her dependency issues later in the reading. Her Loki finger was so curved it significantly overlapped Bragi.

Things do not always go as planned. After only a few minutes it became obvious the reading wasn't making sense to her. "That's not me . . ." she kept saying. "I'm not like that at all."

I had never before experienced a reading that completely missed, but I knew such things happened. I decided to bail out. "I'm sorry," I told her. "It seems that I cannot read you."

"What do you mean?"

"Nobody can read everyone. It's not anyone's fault. I just can't seem to read you."

"You mean my life doesn't fit my hand?"

"Something like that."

Sensing trouble, Big Sis arrived upon the scene. "What is it?"

"He says my life doesn't fit my hand!"

"I'm trying to tell her I can't read her," I explained.

Big Sis pulled up a chair. Little Sis said, "Tell her what you just said."

I repeated the reading. "That's what you do. That's you all right," Big Sis said.

"Oh, okay, go ahead," said Little Sis.

During the course of the reading I had to ask Little Sis her age in order to answer a question of timing. She looked blank! Her older Sis replied, "She's thirty-four years old." Little Sis added, "She's the one who keeps up with stuff like that."

I started to see a pattern. "What do you do for a living?" I asked Little Sis.

"Oh, I work for her." She pointed toward her sister.

"Where do you live?"

"With her. Do you see any happiness in my future, or something?"

I'll admit I was at a loss. How do you tell a hostage how to be happy in captivity?

Little Sis was not mentally ill or subnormal in intelligence. She had simply surrendered control of her life to her sister. I now knew why my reading had been off base. She had almost completely abandoned her identity and behaved as her older sister wanted. She didn't know where she ended and her sister began!

Fifteen minutes was too brief a time to give her much encouragement—but I tried. It was essential that she learned to make decisions for herself. "The happiest people are those who choose a life path and stay with it," I told her. "They pick a direction and follow it. Do you understand what I mean?"

After staring at me blankly for ten full seconds, she responded, "So . . . I should take a walk in the woods more?"

Out of all the possible answers that raced through my mind I finally said, "Yes, I think that would be an excellent place to start . . ." and silently prayed that whatever path she chose would take her as far away from her sister as possible!

Take a Breather!

Whew! This chapter on fingers is the longest one in the book. I'll bet you had no idea how much could be learned just from a quick glance at a person's fingers! Spend a little time reading your friends' and family members' fingers just for the fun of it. In the meantime, please enjoy the Intermission which begins on the following page before plunging into the many aspects of the thumb.

Moderate in counsel should a wise man be
Not brutal and overbearing.
Among the bold the bully will find
Others more bold than he.

THE ELDER EDDA

Intermission

How Tyr Lost His Hand

Take a break and enjoy this terrific story from the Norse mythic tradition!

Loki the Trickster had many children. One was fair of aspect and pleasing to the gods, but not the rest. Everyone knows that while disguised as a mare, Loki gave birth to a lovely foal that grew up to become Odin's swift and powerful steed Sleipnir. However, the three children he sired with the giantess Angerboda were less welcome in Asgard.

One day Loki proudly introduced to the gods his monstrous offspring Hel, Jormangard, and Fenris. The gods shuddered in disgust when they saw Hel, for she was a living woman on one side, fair and lovely, but a decaying corpse on the other! In horror they banished her to Niflheim, where she was to rule over all those who died of old age or of natural causes.

Even less did they welcome Jormangard, who had the aspect of an enormous serpent. They flung him into the sea where he grew so large that he encircled the entire world and held his own tail in his mouth. Jormangard would eventually become so mighty that on the final day of Ragnarok he was destined to slay Thor himself! He eventually became known as the Midgard Serpent.

The third child of Loki was Fenris, a wolf cub. The gods decided to adopt him as a pet. But over time Fenris grew so large that only Tyr, the fearless swordsman, could come close enough to feed him. When Fenris became too dangerous, the gods devised a scheme to bind the savage wolf so that he could do no harm.

The gods decided to trick Fenris into letting them tie him up with strong chains as a test of his strength. Twice he easily burst the colossal fetters the gods bound him with, growling, "Is this the best you can do?"

Odin knew then that the only chain powerful enough to hold the great wolf would have to be forged by magic. He obtained the services of the dwarves, who could make anything, to try and make a rope that would bind Fenris. At the end of a fortnight, the king of the dwarves delivered a light, slender cord to Asgard.

"Will this do the job?" Thor demanded.

The dwarf replied, "Have no doubts on that regard. It will stand the test." Thor tugged and pulled on the cord with all his strength, and it held fast. "I believe you," he concluded. "Bring on the wolf."

Fenris, sniffing suspiciously at the cord, said, "You think this tiny shoestring will hold up against me?" He laughed. "You must be kidding."

Odin replied, "Nevertheless, we would like to see how strong you are, Fenris. Let us bind you with the cord and see if you can break it."

Smelling a trap, Fenris growled, "I'll do so on one condition. One of you must put your hand in my mouth as a guarantee."

The wolf had inherited a good amount of his father's wit. He knew that none of the gods would risk becoming maimed just to trap him! However, Tyr the swordsman stepped forward and announced, "I'll meet your condition, wolf." He offered his left hand to Fenris. "Here is my guarantee."

Fenris snorted, "No. You must guarantee me with your right hand—your sword hand!"

Tyr calmly obliged. "As you wish." And the gods tied Fenris up with the magic cord.

How the wolf did struggle and strain against the magic string! But the more he struggled, the tighter the rope held him. Exhausted, he had to admit the dwarf's cord had beaten him. "You win, Odin," he panted. "Now, untie me!"

Odin refused.

There was a crunching sound, and Tyr pulled away, clutching the stump where his sword hand once was. Eir, the goddess of healing, took Tyr away to bandage the horrible wound while Fenris howled in fury.

The gods left Fenris tied up in a remote corner of the world where his howls shook the skies and slaver ran from his mouth in rivers—but they knew they hadn't seen the last of him. The Norns had decreed that Fenris would be the worst of the gods' enemies. On the twilight of Ragnarok, Fenris would break his fetters, storm Asgard with the gods' other enemies, and take his revenge. He was destined to slay Odin, the All-Father, before being slain himself by Odin's son Vidar.

The recipe used for the magic cord can never be used again, for it was made from the sound of a cat's footstep, the beards of women, the spittle of birds, and the roots of mountains. And this is why, to this day, women do not have beards, nor mountains roots, nor birds spit, and the footstep of a cat makes no sound.

5

Aspects of the Thumb

With the developing mind, the hand developed. With the developing hand, the mind developed . . .

Aristotle,
Metaphysics

The thumb is undoubtedly the most important feature of the hand, dominating almost half of the total surface area. It's certainly our most useful digit. The opposable thumb is what allowed humans to build tools and assume dominance over the earth. In medieval Europe, people would hang their enemies by the thumbs in the belief that breaking their thumbs would break their will. Remove a person's thumb, and the hand is pretty much useless. The thumb is so chock full of information that Indian palmists sometimes do a reading on the thumb alone! After reading this chapter you'll be able to also, if you so desire.

Thor

If the thumb is long and well developed, it shows an overall determination and success at achieving goals. In palmistry, the three phalanges of the thumb represent logic, willpower, and passion. The length and proportion of each phalange tells us how much of each characteristic the person will have (Figure 5.1).

The tip of the thumb, or *Thor,* is the area associated with strength of will and is named for the Norse thunder god. The shape of Thor is very important. For example, a long, tapering thumb tip shows a person with refined sensitivity, someone who can walk down the street and hear the grass grow. A short, blunt thumb shows a type that is outspoken, has strong opinions, and a habit of saying exactly what's on their mind! They do not discourage easy and are good at meeting adversity. Sometimes others find them a bit intimidating. Here's a little quiz: Can you guess what kind of thumb Aunt Eliza has?

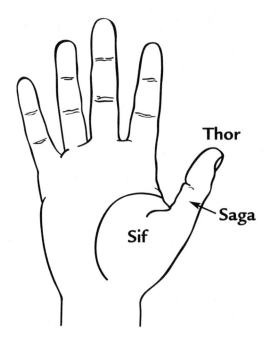

FIGURE 5.1—The three phalanges of the thumb

Thor's Hammer

A noticeably blunt thumb is called *Thor's Hammer* (Figure 5.2), suggesting strength of will and a tendency toward anger and aggression. When this condition is spotted, these people must be cautioned to learn acceptable outlets for their aggression.

An overdeveloped Thor's Hammer can be recognized in a clubbed formation called the "Murderer's Thumb." It shows a tendency toward simmering temper and resentment that can explode into violent action over trivial causes.

Push back against the thumb to determine the degree of stubbornness. If the thumb resists, this type can be quite stubborn when their will is opposed. If the thumb is flexible, they will be more open to new ideas. If the thumb is weak and floppy, they will probably surrender to pressure too easily.

FIGURE 5.2—Thor's Hammer

Saga

The middle phalange, or *Saga*, represents logic and wisdom. When Saga is long, it shows a logical, orderly mind. Such people are usually very good at logic games and crossword puzzles.

If the middle phalange narrows in the center, giving it a wasp-waisted configuration, it is called *Forseti's Spindle* (Figure 5.3). The name *Forseti* means "presiding one," and in the *Poetic Edda* he is "the god that stills all strife." These people have tact, diplomacy, and the ability to mediate, and they can sugarcoat anything.

If a person's thumb shows both stubbornness and diplomacy I say, "You hate to be told you can't do something. If the sign says KEEP OFF THE GRASS, you decide it's a good place to have a picnic. When someone forbids you to do a thing you will smile, nod your head, and do what you intended to do in the first place!" They always grin and agree. These amazing people avoid direct confrontation yet they still manage to have things their way!

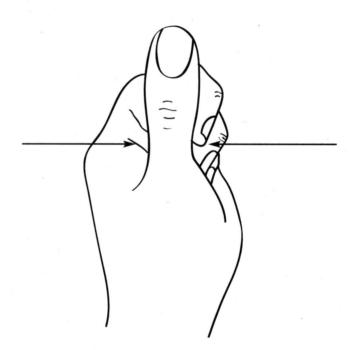

FIGURE 5.3—Forseti's Spindle

Measure for Balance

Measure both phalanges, the tip and the middle, to determine if an imbalance exists. Balance is always important. Too much Thor (the tip of the thumb) makes a person reckless and they will tend to blunder ahead without considering the consequences of their actions. Too much Saga (second phalange) can create unrealistic expectations. Such people will plan far too many activities and habitually have too many irons in the fire! They have a "to do" list that no one person could ever complete in a lifetime.

Sif

The pad of the thumb (Figure 5.4) is named after Thor's wife, Sif. *Sif* has been an area of some controversy among palmists. It is universally agreed that the thumb pad represents an energy battery. Some say this energy is vitality, the ability to enjoy life to the fullest. Others maintain that this area is the sexual

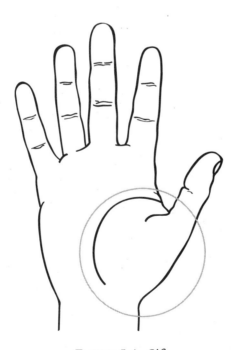

FIGURE 5.4—Sif

storage battery. In my opinion, both schools are correct. Sif governs both physical vitality and erotic energy.

Sif's Energy Levels

Most passionate and sexy people have a large Sif mount (Figure 5.5), showing their delight with all forms of sensual activities. People with large Sifs tend to be gastronomes. Loving good food, good drink, and good sex, their bodies will often be fleshy. Their skin will also be extremely sensitive. Foreplay is very important to people with large Sifs; sometimes more important than the sex act itself.

Small and flat Sif areas (Figure 5.6) are found on people whose sex drives are usually only moderate. They will seem to be tired all the time. Large Sifs indicate more energy and vitality. The size of Sif is variable throughout people's lives, and can increase or decrease depending on their energy level at the time.

Moderate Sifs have variable energy. If involved in an activity they enjoy, their energy is limitless. However, mundane activities tire them out quickly and they tend to procrastinate when confronted with tedious tasks.

Jorda

On the back of the hand behind Sif we find *Jorda,* or the earth mount (Figure 5.7). Although not actually a part of the thumb, it's close enough that you will want to examine it at the same time you look at the thumb. To determine the size of Jorda, ask subjects to hold their hand rigidly straight with the thumb pressed tightly against the side of the hand (like a karate chop). The Jorda mount will now be easier to read. People with large Jordas will have a strong attraction to nature. If small, they will probably prefer the structured existence of city life. Their idea of "roughing it" would be a Holiday Inn without room service!

A lot of Jordas are natural Pagans. In love with nature, they seek out religious practices that place them in contact with Mother Earth. Many of these practices revolve around American Indian and Wiccan beliefs, which emphasize the importance of people's relationship with the planet. Jordas will love

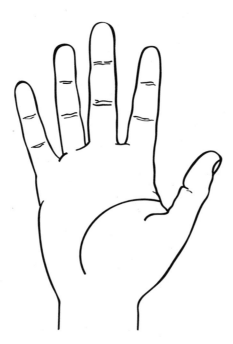

FIGURE 5.5—Large Sif

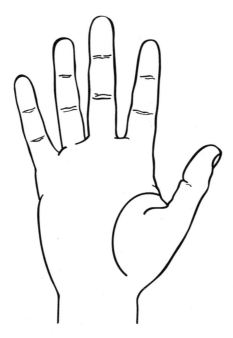

FIGURE 5.6—Small Sif

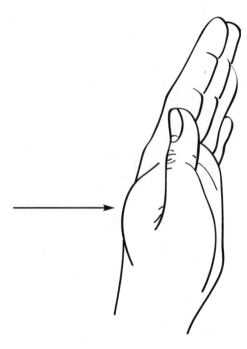

FIGURE 5.7—Jorda

the outdoors and have a greater appreciation than most of a good spring morning, beautiful sunsets, or the spray of water on their face at the beach. Everyone should be fortunate enough to enjoy such abundance. Jordas also enjoy running around in the nude, so don't drop in on them unannounced or you may get an eyeful!

Sif and Lofn

Directly above Sif is the triangular area ruled by Lofn (Figure 5.8), the Norse goddess concerned with sparking passionate love. She had permission from Odin and Frigg to do so even for those who were forbidden to marry. Therefore, overdevelopment in this area reveals an extreme interest in sex. *Lofn* probably rules most sex addicts.

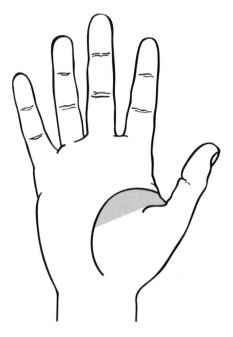

Figure 5.8—Lofn

Lofn is not part of the thumb, but is a mound of flesh adjacent to Sif. When Lofn is puffy and pillowy, you may be dealing with someone who is fickle, unfaithful, and obsessed with sexual conquest. Lots of lines in this area show problems caused by other people in the subject's life.

The Angle of Aegir

Aegir was renowned for his hospitality. He brewed the ale for the gods and threw magnificent parties. The cups in Aegir's hall always magically refilled themselves. *Aegir* represents hospitality, tolerance, and friendliness. To determine the degree of Aegir, ask the subject to hold the thumb of the dominant hand out at a right angle to the palm. The wider the angle, the greater the measure of Aegir's hospitable energy (Figure 5.9). An angle greater than ninety degrees denotes strong Aegir energy.

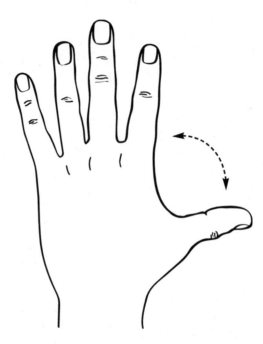

FIGURE 5.9—Wide Aegir

Aegirs love people and can get along with anyone, regardless of their background. Aegirs make excellent hosts and excel at any service that benefits people. They tend to be nonjudgmental and tolerant.

The Critical Angle

When the thumb's angle is well below ninety degrees (Figure 5.10), the Aegir energy is weakened. These subjects will probably be critical, intolerant, and judgmental of others. They will prefer to associate with people who think, feel, and act the same as they do. Since they tend to be a bit aloof and private, they seldom speak their criticisms out loud, but you can bet they think them! People with strong religious or political beliefs often show this "critical angle."

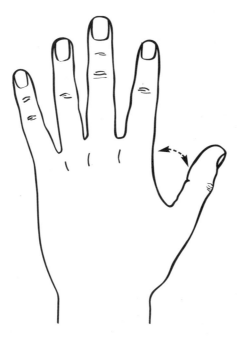

FIGURE 5.10—Narrow Aegir

Idun's Apple

At the base of the thumb near the wrist you will sometimes find a noticeable bump or curve (Figure 5.11). Idun was the goddess who grew the apples that kept the gods eternally young. Goddess of youth, her name means "the rejuvenating one." When present, the apple shows that these people are young at heart, playful, and expressive. No matter what their age, they will bring youthful spontaneity and affection to their life and to everyone around them.

People with Idun's Apples will usually have a good sense of rhythm and enjoy dancing—unless the apple is low on the wrist. Then they will have an off-beat sense of timing which can make them self-conscious and a bit awkward.

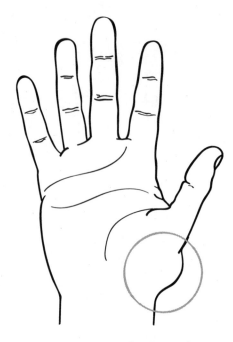

FIGURE 5.11—Idun's Apple

That's All!

I hope you've enjoyed this discussion of the thumb and the Norse deities who rule it. Isn't it amazing how much can be learned from a single digit?

> *Of his knowledge a person should never boast.*
> *Rather, be sparing of speech.*
> *When to his house a wiser man comes*
> *Seldom do those who are silent make mistakes!*
>
> THE ELDER EDDA

6

THE TERRITORIES

The man who stands at a strange threshold
Should be wary before crossing it.

THE WORDS OF THE HIGH ONE

According to ancient Norse legend, the world was divided into several parts. In the beginning was the Void (Ginunga-gap). North of the Abyss was Niflheim, the land of ice. South of the Abyss was Muspelheim, the land of fire. Think of the palm of the hand as a roadmap. The lines (branches) are the pathways. The surface of the palm is the terrain. This terrain is divided into territories, each with its own particular characteristics. These areas are the plains and mounts.

The branches of the World Tree were said to cover the entire universe, therefore the location of these branches influences the energies that flow through them. We will examine this idea further in the next chapter, but before we dive into the branches, let's take a look at the territory upon which they grow.

The Plains

Figure 6.1 shows the major plains of the palm. These are named after the three worlds of Norse legend: Midgard, the world of humans; Muspelheim (*MUZ-pel-hame*), the land of fire; and Niflheim (*NIV-el-hame*), the land of ice. Each territory represents a separate part of our psychological world.

Midgard—The Middle Ground

Located between the branches of the heart (Freya) and the mind (Mimir), Midgard is the "real" world where most of our time and energy is spent. This is the area of worldly matters, relationships, work, and society.

The size of Midgard reveals a person's degree of open-mindedness. Small areas show people who are limited in welcoming new ideas into their world. Wider areas of Midgard indicate more open-minded and experimental people. Their interest in the world is larger, and they show a greater curiosity about the unknown.

The world of Midgard has two extremes (Figure 6.2). The area of Midgard near the first two fingers is *Valhalla,* the home of brave warriors. The area at the opposite end near the heel of the hand is *Jotunheim (YO-tun-hame),* the land of the giants. Firmness in either of these two areas is a sign of courage and valor, although of two different kinds.

If their area of Valhalla is firm to the touch, people will be brave in an understated, modest way. They will be very nice up to a point, but if you cross the line, look out! Soft and polite on the outside, they are solid steel inside. The angrier they get, the quieter and softer their voice will become. You can tell when you're pushing these people near their self-imposed limit by their eyes. A glint of steel, they look like a warrior showing you a couple of inches of sword as a warning. Back off!

Jotunheim was the land of the giants who were a crude, aggressive race. Therefore, firmness in this area shows a more flamboyant style of bravery. I think of these people as enforcers, as you will often find this trait on the hands

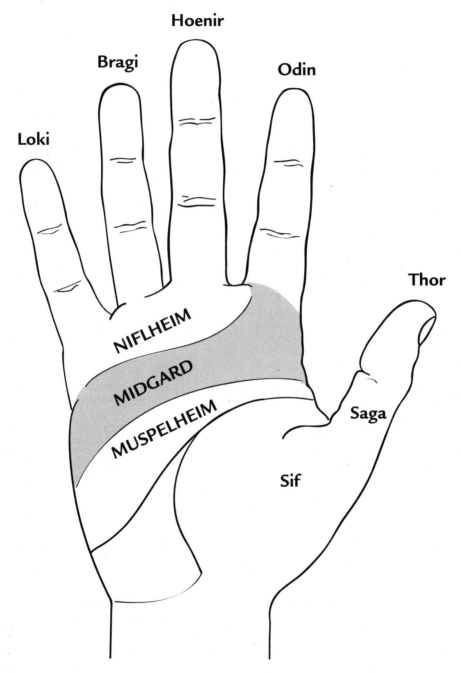

FIGURE 6.1—The major plains of the palm

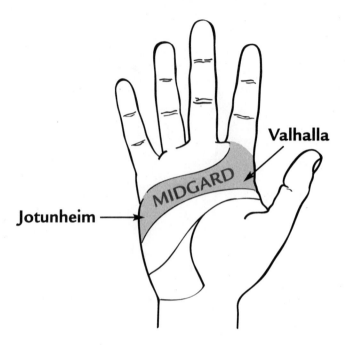

FIGURE 6.2—Valhalla and Jotunheim

of judges, policemen, and military people. Too much development in this area produces a bully.

Of course, softness in both areas shows a person who prefers peace. Excessive softness reveals someone who knuckles under too easily.

Muspelheim—The World of Fire

Muspelheim is the world between the head branch (Mimir) and the area of instinctive needs (Sif) (Figure 6.3). This territory represents the programming we receive from our parents and society. It starts on the thumb side of the hand and spreads out toward the wrist.

People with areas that start small and rapidly expand as they move across the hand will be homebodies and fond of tradition. Home and hearth will mean a great deal to them. They will probably know a lot of history about their hometown, family, or ethnic origin. They will not rush into things. They accept change

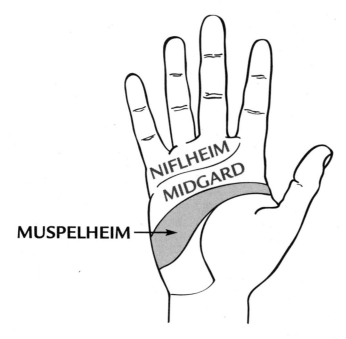

FIGURE 6.3—Muspelheim

as long as it occurs gradually enough so they can adapt to it. These people are usually very successful in their chosen fields, since they can plan for the future and work for the long term.

Sometimes the area narrows along the length of the palm. These people will break away from their early programming and become more self-directed the older they become. The area narrows because of a large Sif area, so they will possess a great deal of vigor. Since this area is the land of fire, they will live life with gusto and passion. Their motto is "Moderation is for monks— take BIG bites!"

Niflheim—Land of the Spirits

Niflheim is the world between the heart branch (Freya) and the roots of the fingers, which represent the spirit (Figure 6.4). Niflheim was the Norse land of the dead, so we associate this area with the spirit.

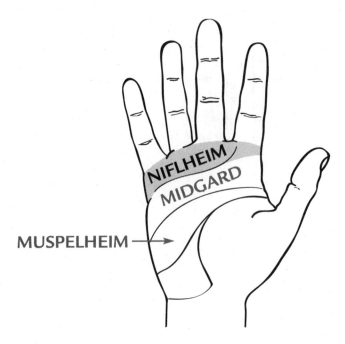

FIGURE 6.4—Niflheim

Niflheim represents our higher aspirations and self-development. People with wide Niflheims will be driven toward self-improvement, set lofty goals, and will achieve them through steadfast effort. They will quite often have a strong spirituality that sustains them in times of woe.

People with narrow Niflheim areas will be content to get by, never really attaining their full potential. Good examples of this are people who are very intelligent, yet insist on working menial jobs or who don't do as well as they could in school.

Vertical twigs in Niflheim give the person a sensitive, healing touch. They give great back rubs!

The Mounts

The mounts are raised areas or bumps on certain parts of the palm. They are named after the Norse gods who rule them (Figure 6.5). Mounts are storage

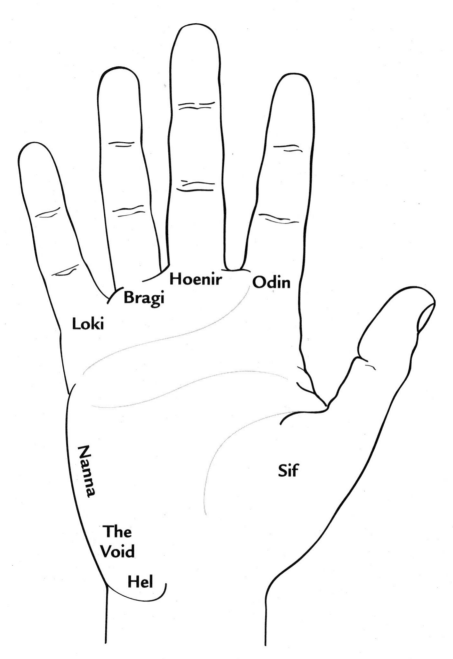

FIGURE 6.5—The mounts

batteries, stockpiles of energy that fuel certain aspects of the personality. Most palmists believe that the mounts show what a person is happiest doing. I tend to agree.

You are already familiar with the Jorda mount from your study of the thumb. Jorda is unique in that it is the only mount found on the back of the hand. You'll recall it gives a person great enjoyment and appreciation of nature. The other mounts are equally revealing.

Reading the Mounts

This is the easiest part of hand analysis. The mounts have the same energy as the corresponding finger. If the mount is large, it strengthens the finger's energy. If small, its contribution is minimal.

Location of the Mounts

Four of the mounts are named after the fingers under which they lie. For example, under the Odin finger lies the *mount of Odin,* and so on. The other mounts—Nanna, Hel, and the Void—are located along the heel of the hand. We will look at these in a moment.

Because a mount strengthens the energy of a finger, a strong mount can compensate for a weak finger. For example, a large Loki mount will take the curse off of a weak Loki finger and give the person a boost of communication energy.

Since the meaning of each mount is similar to its corresponding finger, you have already learned to interpret most of them. Just remember that the mounts show what we enjoy doing. People with large mounts of Odin will thrive on positions of authority, decision-making, and any job where they get to tell others what to do.

People with large mounts of Hoenir will be drawn into areas such as preaching, teaching, training, or writing. They will love long discussions about spirituality, philosophy, and psychology, and will be good at "reading between the lines."

Well-developed Bragi mounts give people much success in the fields of art, literature, fashion, or design. They will find their greatest enjoyment in creating things, designing, fixing or remodeling homes, writing, painting, sculpting, or any other craft.

Mounts of Loki denote born salespeople and communicators who will love to tell stories and jokes. They will be naturally gifted with a silver tongue and are very resourceful. If you were to drop them in the Sahara and returned in a week to collect their bones, they'll have managed to set up a lemonade stand. Aunt Eliza says they can sell you your own socks, and when you bend down to put them on, they'll steal your shoes and sell them back to you too!

The Mount of Nanna

On the heel of the hand is the *mount of Nanna* (Figure 6.6), the Norse moon goddess. The moon is traditionally associated with empathy, intuition, and public service. People with large sweeping curves to the edge of their hands have strong Nanna energies. This makes them profoundly empathic, which

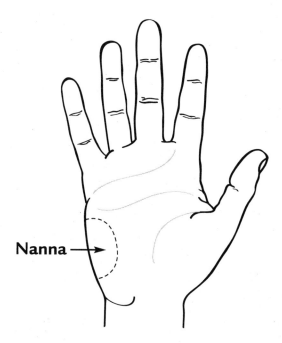

FIGURE 6.6—Nanna

means they are sensitive to the emotional state of those around them. As wonderful as this gift can be, it's usually a mixed blessing. Empathic people can be overwhelmed by the power of other people's emotions.

If the Nanna person is involved in a career helping others deal with emotional problems, well and good. However, they frequently find themselves surrounded by family and friends who constantly yearn for the Nanna's healing attention. A lot of Nannas ask me, "Why do all my friends and family members have so many problems?" It may not be true that their friends have more problems than normal; the Nanna energy tends to bring it out in the open. Even normally taciturn people will open up to a Nanna.

Auras act as electromagnets, attracting and repelling other people. Nannas' auras are warm, snuggly, and nurturing. These auras act as beacons to attract the emotionally needy to the empath. You can see how this can be both a gift and a curse!

Empaths have been described as "emotional sponges," and I think this description is quite apt. When an empathic person is in a roomful of fun, happy people, they actually get a high from the emotional energy. However, when around angry or depressed people, they feel completely drained. It's important for the empath to avoid such "energy vampires."

It's interesting to watch how an empath rides the emotional wave of those around them. For example, if they're watching a comedy at home, they may react quietly or not at all. But if you put them in a theater full of people, they'll laugh along until they hurt themselves!

Empaths often carry around the emotional baggage of others and mistake it for their own. They will feel drained and depressed but not know why. Nannas can accidentally pick up the negative energy charge from people around them. These foreign energies are called *exogenetic emotions,* since they originate from outside the individual.

My friend Ron Martin says this is like someone approaching you at a party and handing you a bunch of broken glass. "Hold on to this for me, would you?" they say and move on, leaving you standing there with a handful of slivers. Empaths must learn to refuse this emotional onslaught. Unfortunately, this is difficult for them to do. They hate to disappoint anybody and will actually feel guilty when they act in their own self-defense.

The Void

Below Nanna lies the *Void* (Ginunga-gap) (Figure 6.7). This territory represents the primal beginning, the vast resources of the unconscious mind, and knowledge brought in from past lives.

Think of the mind as having two layers. The top layer, the one readily accessible to us, is the conscious mind. This is the part of us that we assume is logical, rational, and in control—the part of our mind that "thinks." Beneath this superficial conscious mind lies a deeply buried, irrational, and instinctive component that is the real boss. This part of us is so mysterious that we cannot adequately describe it. Like the Tao, any description would be a falsehood. Beyond logic, beyond rationality, and beyond reason lies the Void. You can call

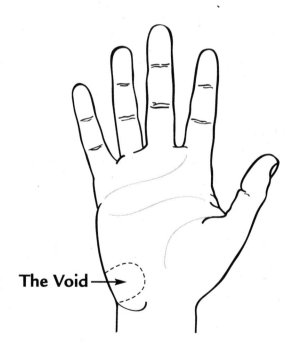

The Void

FIGURE 6.7—The Void

it our instinctive level, but this would be a tremendous oversimplification of the unconscious mind.

People with large Voids have strongly powered unconscious resources. This holds especially true if the Norn's Thread (see chapter 8) grows from this area. They have vast reserves of mystical energy and they are clairvoyant, or able to know things about people and places without logical thought. They can touch inanimate objects and receive psychic impressions from them. They experience déjà vu, the mysterious knowledge of a place they have never been to before, and they have vivid dreams that usually come true.

People with large Voids can tap into the unconscious mind while sleeping. Often they go to bed with a tough problem on their minds and wake up the next morning knowing exactly what to do. Large Voids can indicate truly gifted people, people who do not think like the rest of us.

Unfortunately, these wonderful abilities lie dormant in most people, even in those with a well-developed Void. I always try and encourage them to explore and develop their hidden potential. Once discovered, these hidden talents can develop with amazing speed.

Hel

According to Norse mythology, Loki's first wife was the evil giantess Angerboda. The offspring of this union were Fenris, the giant wolf that one day would destroy Odin; the Midgard serpent Jormangard; and Hel, the queen of the dead. She was depicted as a living person on her right side and a corpse on her left. Her domain was Niflheim and her hall was called *Elvidnir,* which means "misery." You can tell when *Hel* is large mainly because it deforms the *Serpent,* a bandlike "bracelet" that curves around the wrist (Figure 6.8).

Hel represents the darkness beneath the conscious mind where all fears, anxieties, morbid thoughts, and phobias are spawned. Fortunately, Hel is usually active only for short periods of time, triggered by astrological influences, lunar phases, or excessive stress. During periods when Hel is strong, people with large Hels will be especially sensitive to darker energies, and at times their thoughts may even turn morbid. Usually these negative thoughts have little or

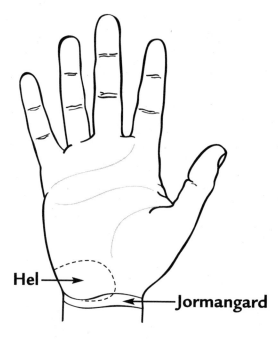

FIGURE 6.8—Hel

no basis in reality, and can be easily dismissed simply by concentrating on the positive aspects of life.

Hel energy can cause a person to experience a free-floating anxiety or sense of dread that the mind attempts to project onto the real world. Rather than surrender to gloomy dejection, it is far preferable to learn to redirect negative thinking into more positive channels.

If you have a large area of Hel, do not despair. Remember, the darkness ever flees the light. By practicing positive imagery and contacting your higher spirit, you'll find Hel's influence easily overcome. "Yea, though I walk through the Shadow of the Valley of Death, I will fear no evil, for Thou art with me. . . ."

Final Thoughts

We all probably have a little bit of Hel in us, so above all we must resist the tendency to blow small setbacks or rejections out of proportion. Hel can cause a person see things as being worse than they really are. This is purely illusion, so we must learn to let it go and see the reality of life: that the world is filled with countless blessings!

Interestingly enough, development of the Hel mount usually gives a person an interest in antiquities, archaeology, and ancient cultures. Perhaps a good antidote to Hel's negative side is to dwell among the wisdom of the ancients studying Egyptology, Wicca, Druidism, Buddhism, or Nordic legend!

But my Aunt Eliza's advice is probably the best—it's as good as any psychologist's I ever heard: "When worrisome thoughts come to trouble you, tell 'em to go back to hell where they came from!"

If you know a friend you can fairly trust
Go often to his house.
Grass and brambles quickly grow
Upon the untrodden path.

                                            THE POETIC EDDA

7

THE BRANCHES
OF YGGDRASIL

. . . I know an Ash-Tree, named Yggdrasil.
Sparkling showers are shed on its leaves
That drip dew onto the world below.
By Urd's well it waves, forever green.

THE SONG OF THE SYBIL

When most people hear the word *palmistry,* they automatically think of the lines and creases in the palm of the hand. But as you know by now, there's a great deal more to hand reading than merely looking at the lines in the palm!

In runic palmistry we see these lines as branches of Yggdrasil, the World Tree. The branches act as conduits of the life force that flows from Yggdrasil and which channel our energy to various aspects of our lives. The quality and form of these branches reveal how we use this energy.

The Tree of Life

According to Norse mythology, Yggdrasil (*IG-dra-sil*) was an enormous ash tree that supported the universe. One of its roots extended into Niflheim, the underworld; another into Jotunheim, land of the giants; and the third into Asgard, home of the gods.

At its base were three wells: the Well of Fate, from which the tree was watered by the Norns; the Roaring Kettle in which dwelt Nidhogg, the monster that gnawed at the tree's roots; and Mimir's Well, the source of all wisdom. After Ragnarok (doomsday), the World Tree, though badly shaken, would be the source of all new life.

Think of the lines in the palm as the roots and branches of the world tree Yggdrasil. The roots begin near the edges of the hand and spread across the palm, where they become branches.

Look at the chart and familiarize yourself with the three major branches: *Freya*, the goddess of love and marriage, governs the heart; *Sif* controls the life path; and *Mimir* rules the head. There are many more branches that we will look at later, but these are the main three.

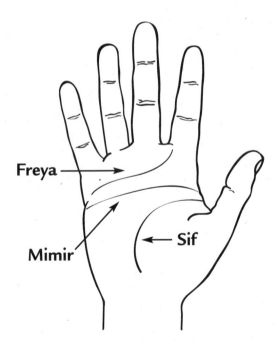

FIGURE 7.1—The major branches of
Yggdrasil

The Branch of Sif

We've already learned that the pad of the thumb is Sif's domain
is easy to spot as it is the boundary of this area (Figure 7.2). Sif's b
a wide arc around the pad of the thumb. In classical palmistry it i
the *life line*, since it is said to measure a person's life energy. This is
more enduring pieces of fiction about the life line (or branch of ﹖
know it), so be prepared. As soon as word gets out that you're studyir.
istry, a great line of people will form, all of them shoving their hands
your nose and demanding, "Tell me how long I'm going to live!" Of cou﹐
one can do this, but the branch of Sif can tell much about the quality of ﹐
son's life.

Carefully examine the termination of the branch of Sif where it spreads
limbs near the wrist. If the branch has a single ending, the person is w﹐
rooted and enjoys staying in one spot. However, if the branch presents two o

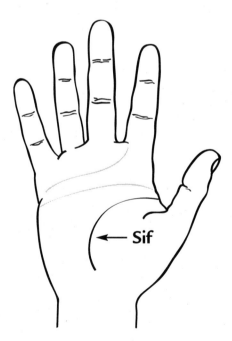

FIGURE 7.2—Sif's branch

more forks, that person will be a restless spirit and have a strong desire to travel.

When Sif's branch travels close to the thumb, the Sif pad will contain less energy. These people are a bit tired all the time. They require frequent rest breaks and like to sleep a lot. It's necessary for people with small Sifs to take especially good care of themselves and work on increasing their energy level.

People whose Sif branches go well out into the palm will have almost limitless energy and the desire to stay active. They will love challenges and anything that gives them the opportunity to set large goals and achieve them. Their sex drive will be strong, as a wide, sweeping Sif branch is only found on those with a large Sif joint. Don't flirt with them unless you mean business!

Sif's Life Path

Often you will see a Sif branch that breaks either inward toward the thumb or outward toward the heel of the hand. These breaks show changes in life path direction.

If the Sif branch breaks inward (Figure 7.3), these people will become calmer and more conservative as they grow older. When they retire, they will probably enjoy a quiet life, preferring to stay at home, watch TV, or putter around in the garden.

If the Sif branch breaks outward (Figure 7.4), these people will become more energetic and independent as they mature. It's almost as though their spirit becomes younger as their body ages. They often begin second careers late in life, sometimes starting their own businesses or going back to school.

Twigs on Sif

Lots of twigs shooting off of Sif's branch show a tendency to scatter a person's life force all over the place. These people have difficulty achieving big goals because their energy is wasted on a great many trivial matters. Often, they are so occupied with the minutiae of their daily existence that they can't see the forest for the trees. They must learn to simplify their life in order to conserve their energy for the things that need to be done.

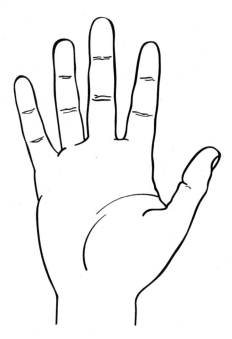

FIGURE 7.3—An inward break of the
Sif branch

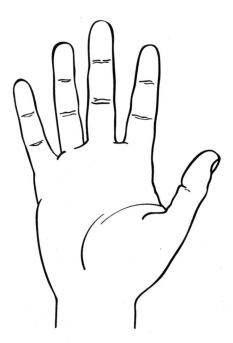

FIGURE 7.4—An outward break of the
Sif branch

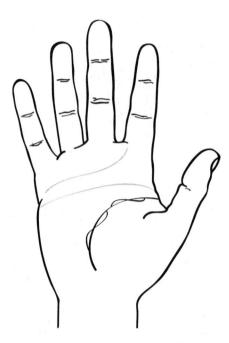

FIGURE 7.5—Leaves on Sif's branch

Leaves on the Branch

Sometimes you will notice oval or island-shaped areas on the branch (Figure 7.5). These are called *leaves* and represent life lessons, which is the metaphysical way of saying "hard times." Leaves found on Sif's branch represent times when life energy became blocked through illness, accident, or traumatic life circumstances. The person's life was literally on hold. If you stay with a frustrating situation too long and begin to feel like you're stuck there forever, you will probably develop a leaf on Sif's branch.

The Branch of Mimir

Mimir's branch provides clues about our mental processes. Mimir was the god of wisdom and knowledge, so we look at this branch to find out how a person thinks. Mimir plants his roots on the thumb side of the hand and grows out-

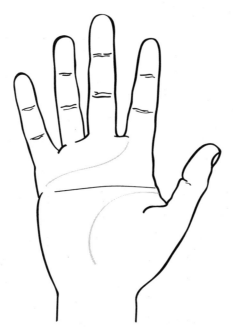

FIGURE 7.6—Mimir's branch

ward toward the heel (Figure 7.6). People whose branch is entangled with Sif will usually have a careful approach to life. They will think things through before acting. If leaves appear in this area it can represent unresolved child-hood traumas.

The Gap

The wider the gap between Mimir and Sif (Figure 7.7), the bolder the person will be in speech and action. They'll fret under a disciplined upbringing and resist parental control. Most people with a moderate gap aren't strictly dare-devils, but they will enjoy fast speeds and physical activities. They also tend to talk first and think later, so quite often they can be strongly outspoken. Usually this gets worse the older they become, and when they are elderly they turn into lovable eccentrics like my Aunt Eliza.

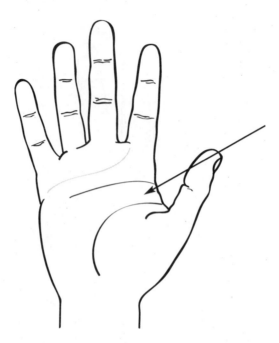

FIGURE 7.7—A large gap between
Mimir's and Sif's branches

Curved or Straight?

Mimir's branches that curve toward the wrist (Figure 7.8) show people with
good imaginations and creative abilities. Too strong a curve makes them
dreamers; that is, they will have excellent ideas, but these ideas are most likely
to remain in their head. Curved Mimirs need mental stimulation in their jobs
or they will escape into daydreams and fantasies. Their work in life is to learn
practical ways of making their ideas really happen. Sometimes their goals and
aspirations can be unrealistic.

Mimir's branches that are straight show people who are technical thinkers.
Their minds will tend to be orderly and logical. Such people are good with
numbers and technical professions. Imagination and creativity are not their
strong points. Excellent problem-solvers, they usually see things in black-and-
white terms. Once they make a decision, all gray areas disappear. These people

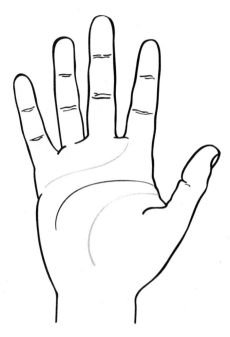

FIGURE 7.8—Curved Mimir's branch

follow logical thought to its conclusion and are hard to move once they've made up their mind. Sometimes they come across as know-it-alls, but in their case it's probably true.

Curved and *Straight?*

Sometimes you'll come across a Mimir branch that forks at the end (Figure 7.9). Since one fork will be straight and the other curved, you're looking at someone who can think both logically and creatively. Truly, they can see both sides of any issue.

This is an important sign for anyone who wants to create a product. A writer or painter must have both the creative inspiration to generate an idea as well as the technical skill to pull it off. For example, in order to write a book you must be creative enough to have something worth saying, and the knowledge of language to write well. If you paint, you have to know design and color theory, and

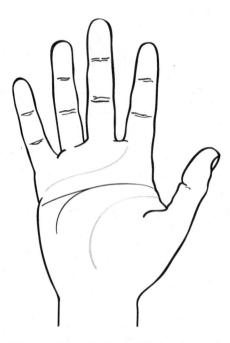

FIGURE 7.9—Forked Mimir's branch

so on. Forked Mimirs are usually masters of efficiency—they figure out easier and better ways to do things. Think of creativity in a practical sense.

On occasion you will spot someone with a trident, or triple fork! These people bring a unique perspective to anything they do. I tell them, "Most people see things either one or two ways. You see things three ways—the right way, the wrong way, and your way!" They always agree. This formation is doubly blessed at it forms the rune *Eolh* (ᛉ), which we'll study in detail in Part II.

The third fork dips further into the part of the hand that represents the subconscious. This allows people with tridents to add a special dream dimension to their world. They see possibilities where others would say none exist. They have an off-the-wall sense of humor, and often find laughter in situations where other people do not. A writer with a trident would probably create good fantasies or science fiction.

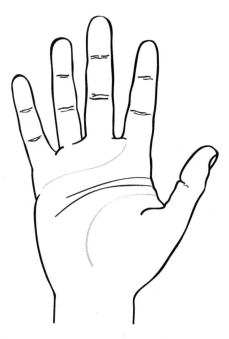

FIGURE 7.10—Double Mimir's
branch

Two Heads?

Even more rare than the trident will you find a double Mimir's branch (Figure 7.10). This is like having two differing personalities trapped in one brain. These people can literally be of two minds about a subject, making quick decisions difficult. Often these two personalities are at odds with each other. The famous English palmist Cheiro had a double "head line," which he showed to everybody he met. Cheiro said this was proof of people who lived "double lives." Sometimes it can mean they know twice as much as anyone else, or that they juggle two careers.

Leaves on the Branch of Mimir

Leaves on Mimir (Figure 7.11) can represent times in people's lives when they were intellectually stifled. Good examples would be working at a job that's

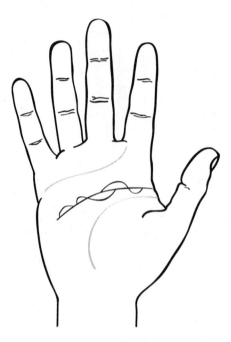

FIGURE 7.11—Leaves on Mimir's
branch

beneath one's intellectual level, or being in a relationship where communication is impossible.

Leaves can also indicate injuries to the head or a high fever in childhood, but this falls into the medical domain and is none of our business. If many leaves appear on the branch, the person may have difficulty concentrating.

Breaks in Mimir can indicate psychological traumas—such as grief or fright—from which the person hasn't recovered fully. Often these traumas date from early childhood. I always urge people with this sign to work through the trauma. If necessary, I refer them to a grief counselor or psychotherapist.

Length of Mimir

Long Mimirs have long attention spans, while short Mimirs have shorter ones. I find that the longer the branch of Mimir, the deeper the person's capacity for concentration. If they like to read, they will immerse themselves in a book for

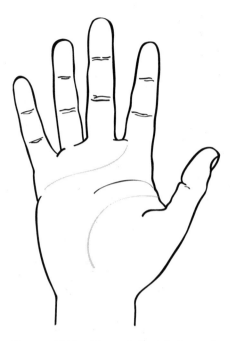

FIGURE 7.12—Short Mimir's branch

hours with no conception of what's going on around them. They will be able to absorb large amounts of information in a short amount of time. Long Mimirs like to collect a great deal of information before they make up their minds, so don't expect a fast decision from them. But if a task requires laserlike focus, they are the one to go to. If the branch is very long, these people may be a bit obsessive. In an argument they can really bear down on a point!

Those with a shorter Mimir (Figure 7.12) do best when they take frequent rest breaks from study or learning. But don't ever assume that a short Mimir implies a lack of intelligence. Their attention span may be shorter, but they grasp an idea very quickly. They are also more spontaneous and adaptable to change than those with long Mimirs. They like to jump into the middle of things and finish them quickly.

I imagine two people shopping, one with a long Mimir and the other with a short one. The long Mimir is looking at every item in the store while the short

Mimir is fretting with impatience, "Get it and let's go!" In other words, when dealing with a long Mimir, don't hold your breath.

The Well of Mimir

Before we leave Mimir, we need to examine one more aspect of the palm. The center of the palm is Mimir's Well, which can be measured by asking subjects to cup their hands in a claw shape as though holding a softball. The palm of the hand will exhibit a cuplike depression in the middle. If the well is deep, the person will drink deeply from the cup of wisdom. Their talents lie in teaching, advising, and counseling.

The Branch of Freya

Freya's branch grows from the edge of the hand and can end anywhere under the first two fingers (Figure 7.13). Since Freya was the goddess of love and marriage, her branch rules over the emotions. Ideally, it should be smoothly curved and terminate exactly between Odin and Hoenir, indicating a balance between giving and receiving love.

Emotional Expression

Branches that are long and curved and end between the first two fingers show people who will be hopeless romantics. They will be ruled by their emotions. The larger the curve, the more energy the branch can sustain. A strong Freya cannot hide their feelings. No matter how hard they try, their face will give them away. You can always tell when they're up to something!

Curved Freyas love romance. They fall in love often and deeply. This passionate roller coaster ride is a lot of fun, but it can put plenty of wear and tear on the heart.

Leaves found on Freya's branch (Figure 7.14) indicate heartbreak and disappointment in love. Each leaf represents a separate episode. Some Freya branches have so many leaves they resemble a braided chain!

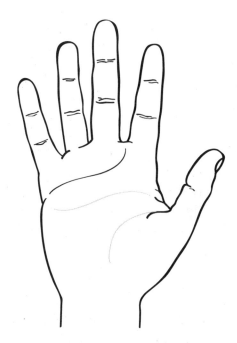

FIGURE 7.13—Freya's branch

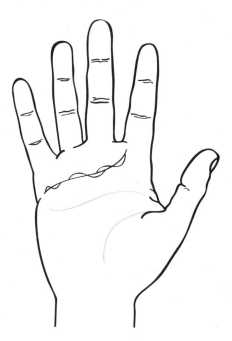

FIGURE 7.14—Leaves on Freya's
branch

Sometimes you will see a number of short lines on Freya's branch. These are called *Twigs of Flirtation*. These people like to experience a variety of lovers and tend to be teases. Remember President Carter's admission that he "lusted in his heart?" People with these twigs may not ever act on these urges, but they certainly think about it.

Breaks in Freya's branch can show periods of emotional isolation. These lonely periods may or may not have been of the person's choosing. Don't assume they were necessarily bad experiences either. Sometimes we need to be alone for a while to get to know ourselves better.

Romantic Strategies

Curved Freyas can be a bit fantasy-prone and naïve, refusing to see the dark side of their beloved until it's too late. When initiating a new relationship, they are often so swept up by the experience that they ignore the advice of friends (and the alarm bells in their head) until disaster hits. In retrospect, they always say they should have known better.

A male curved Freya will court his beloved with flowers and dinner, while a female curved Freya will be a sucker for this romantic treatment. Curved Freyas love to embrace each other and take long walks on the beach holding hands.

Unfortunately, naïve Freyas are often victims of their own romantic notions. Manipulative people can easily take advantage of them by telling them what they want to hear and playing their own emotions against them. Aunt Eliza says, "The problem with wearing your heart on your sleeve is that people wipe their noses on it!"

Conflict Between Mimir and Freya

Sometimes you will see a curved Freya and a straight Mimir on the same hand. This indicates that a type whose head and heart do not agree. The romantic heart suggests idealistic adventures, but the practical mind dismisses them. Thus, these people often talk themselves out of fun adventures and growth experiences, saying, "Maybe some day."

Sometimes the situation is just the opposite. The idealistic heart will fall for a dangerous person while the practical head sends out loud alarm bells. The heart ignores the head but later on wishes it hadn't. Live and learn.

The Poker Face

Straight Freya branches (Figure 7.15) show people who are good at hiding their emotions. However, don't ever make the mistake of assuming they don't have feelings. These individuals are the most intense of the lot. They feel things strongly but are not eager to express their feelings. Because of this tendency, they are a great deal more sensitive than you would think from their outward appearance. They consider it wise not to reveal too much of themselves to others and will only tell you what you need to know. Excellent at keeping secrets, straight Freyas always have an ace up their sleeve, secret knowledge they hoard until needed.

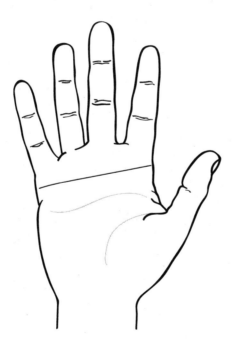

FIGURE 7.15—Straight Freya's branch

Straight Freyas tend to bottle up resentment for a long time and act like nothing is bothering them. Then some small event will catalyze the storehouse of rage and out it will come! If the Odin finger is long, the person will thunder and rage like a tornado. Also like a tornado, the storm will quickly pass and the weather will be calm for a while.

Relationship Patterns

Those with long, straight Freya branches can be possessive and a bit insecure, requiring constant proof of their partner's loyalty. They are extremely devoted, however, and remain with their beloved through thick and thin.

Straight Freyas are attracted to the sexual and physical aspects of a person and are fond of physically attractive people. They like someone who looks good in tight jeans! The straight Freyas are also the most demanding of lovers, requiring the entire package—emotional, physical, and sexual satisfaction.

Eir's Twig

The Freya branch that ends close to the second finger is known as *Eir's Twig* (Figure 7.16), which reveals a desire to help others. Eir (*yeer*) was the goddess of healing who taught the healing arts to women in ancient Scandinavia. Sometimes the twig actually travels up into the finger itself, amplifying the giving energy. Compassionate and giving, people who show this trait tend to devote their lives to others. It is said that Mother Teresa was possessed of an Eir's Twig. Such people naturally want to help and heal people.

Eirs give and give and give, rarely thinking of themselves. It is difficult for Eirs to ask for help even when needed. On the other hand, they find it hard to refuse when asked to donate their time and energy to others. People with an Eir that is too strong will give their life away in bits and pieces, never giving themselves a second thought. The psychological term for this behavior—where another person's needs are more important to you than your own—is *codependency*.

Unfortunately, this giving tendency is seized upon by selfish people who will take advantage of Eirs. They will take until there is nothing left to gain,

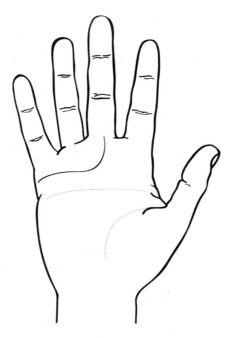

FIGURE 7.16—Eir's Twig

then abruptly disappear. Therefore it is essential that Eirs learn to say no, a very difficult thing for them to do.

Eirs naturally gravitate toward careers that allow them to express their humanitarian instincts, usually becoming nurses, teachers, therapists, and social workers. If they do not help people in their day jobs, they tend to do it with everyone around them, often becoming the "Dear Abby" of their social group.

Frigg's Twig

When Freya's branch terminates under the first finger (Figure 7.17), the person's love is turned inward. The first finger (Odin) represents the ego, so when the branch ends here, the Odin energy fuels the heart. For this reason we call this formation *Frigg's Twig*, after Odin's wife, the queen of the gods. And indeed, people with this branch are usually "princes" or "princesses"!

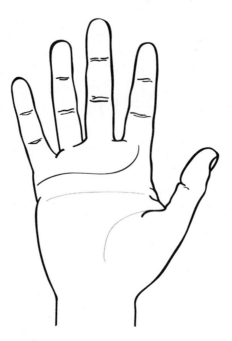

FIGURE 7.17—Frigg's Twig

The Odin energy causes people with Frigg's Twigs to become a bit self-absorbed. They will love being the center of attention. Willful, and at times demanding, they are among the most attractive people in the world. They just ooze charisma.

These people must always feel they are in control of a relationship. Quite often Friggs attempt to instruct everyone around them how they should think and feel, and become resentful when others refuse to accept their advice.

Friggs are usually a bit jealous. Frigg was a jealous goddess, constantly nagging Odin about his numerous love affairs. In fact, the opening act of Wagner's opera *Das Rheingold* finds Frigg chastising Odin for his many infidelities. One of my friends is married to a beautiful woman with a strong Frigg branch. He once told me, "If we're walking around at the mall and I just *look* at another woman, I never hear the end of it!" Of course, Frigg's Twigs are found on the hands of both men and women.

In moderation, Frigg energy gives people self-confidence and the ability to look after themselves. In excess, it creates people who thrive on the admiration of others. It is certainly possible to enjoy a satisfying relationship with a Frigg. As long as you realize that their needs will always come first, you will get along just fine. They love to be pampered and spoiled and usually have expensive tastes. Friggs can learn to be more giving if they put their minds to it, it's just a little more difficult for them. But who said that life was easy?

As readers, we must learn to be tactful. When I see Frigg's Twig, I tell them, "You like to be in control of your relationships, and even in marriage you will never be too dependent on the other person. You like to feel loved and cared for, but not smothered. You love having people around you, but sometimes you need to be left alone to introspect and recharge your batteries. Other times you like to be pampered and spoiled. You're protective of what's yours, and may be a bit possessive in a relationship. You like to know that your lover sees you as something special." They usually agree.

Of course, Aunt Eliza handles Friggs differently. She tells them they're spoiled brats who need to get out of their own back pockets! "Why don't you think of somebody else for a change?" she asks them. When I suggested that she could be a tad more diplomatic, she told me that at her age, she didn't have time to beat around the bush. She wields a machete; I prefer a powder puff.

Cherish those near you, never be
The first to break with a friend.
Care eats him who can no longer
Open his heart to another.

THE WORDS OF THE HIGH ONE

8

THE THREADS
OF THE NORNS

*Macbeth: "How now, you secret, black and midnight hags? What is't
you do?"*
Witches: "A deed without a name."

WILLIAM SHAKESPEARE,
MACBETH

The Norns were the goddesses of fate. They determined the courses
of people's lives and controlled the factors that went into shaping
their personalities. They were also known as the *Wyrd* (pronounced
"weird"). At the moment of people's births the three Norn sisters
(*Urd, Verdandi,* and *Skuld*) wove together the threads of their destiny
and tossed the thread out into the world. In the *Elder Edda,* it says
of the Norns:

> *Laws they gave,*
> *Lives they chose*
> *For the children of men,*
> *The destiny of men.*

Other schools of palmistry have called this trait the *fate line*
in the belief that people's fates were preordained and this line

represented their inevitable future. Modern palmists have rejected this idea, believing futures are created, not predicted. Therefore, the Norn's Thread shows the direction of people's lives, revealing the influences that determined the development of their personalities.

Norse legend tells us that the three sisters often worked against each other. One of the Norns would give someone a gift—a unique skill, talent, or ability that was intended to enrich the person's life. Out of spite, one of the other sisters would transform the gift into a curse!

We see the results of this sibling rivalry at work in the real world. We're told by talented artists, empaths, and clairvoyants that their gifts are often pains in the neck. We've all seen how an active imagination can be both a blessing and a curse. As Grandma used to say, "Ability is responsibility."

The Norn's Thread usually begins somewhere near the wrist of the hand and winds upward toward the fingers (Figure 8.1). However, this is one of the most volatile areas in the hand and will take a little practice to identify. In my opinion it's one of the most important details found in the hand, so any time spent learning about it is well invested.

You will discover early on that very few people have a textbook Norn's Thread. A good way to check the line is to examine its ending point. While the Norn's Thread can begin anywhere in the hand, it must always end under Hoenir (the second finger). If it ends under any of the other fingers it isn't a true Norn's Thread. To add to the confusion, some people will have several Norn's Threads—including some short ones—and some will have none at all.

Masters of Their Fate

At the turn of the twentieth century it was commonly believed a person lacking a Norn's Thread was doomed to failure. This is not so, in my opinion. I've observed that people with no Norn's Thread are motivated, self-made people who create their own destinies. They usually don't believe in fate and are determined to create their future with their own two hands. So it's not a bad sign if the Norn's Thread is missing altogether, although those with a short thread may be late bloomers or early quitters, preferring play over work.

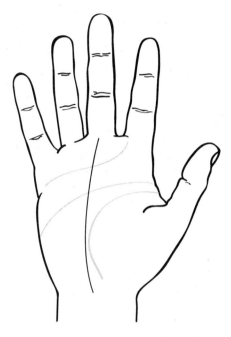

FIGURE 8.1—Norn's Thread

Where the thread begins is vitally important. We will look at several examples as we go along, and hopefully the diagrams will help you understand the dynamics of the Norn's Thread.

The Intrepid Explorer of Alternatives

When the Norn's Thread begins in the heel of the hand (Figure 8.2), it indicates a type who will test established boundaries and march to a different drum. Within the family unit they often feel as though they are from a different planet, as they operate on a different mental level than those around them. These feelings of isolation will plague them until they realize that they truly are different and learn to celebrate their differences. Often they find themselves in unusual professions, such as palm reading or alternative therapy.

You will notice this variation of the thread begins in the Void. This means that these people's personalities are created by the mystical forces that rule

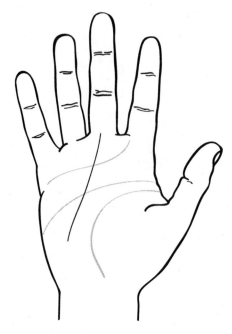

FIGURE 8.2—Norn's Thread
beginning in the heel of the hand

them. They are motivated by different forces than the rest of society and will always be the ones to point out hypocrisy, ask embarrassing questions, and read the Bible looking for loopholes!

The most significant thing I can tell you about this particular thread is that I see a great many at psychic fairs, but when I'm doing readings at a corporate party I may only see one or two during the entire night. They are very rare people indeed.

The People Pleaser

Norn's Threads that grow out of Sif (Figure 8.3) indicate people who are primarily concerned with pleasing others. You can assume that the influence of the family and society was very strong when they were young. Often these people

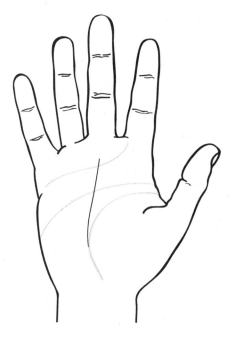

FIGURE 8.3—Norn's Thread
growing out of Sif's branch

will evolve toward a greater independence as they mature. When this is the case, the Norn's Thread swings farther away from Sif as it approaches the fingers. I tell them, "In the past you were primarily concerned with pleasing others, and if someone said they didn't like something about you, you would worry yourself to death. But now you are listening more to the inner voice that tells you who you really are. This is a good sign that you're heading in the right direction." Aunt Eliza would add, "Just learn to say 'To hell with what other people think!'"

You can see from these examples that the farther away the thread drifts from Sif, the less impact social convention has on a person. Sif represents the influence of family and society, while the Void represents the Great Unknown. All your life you're balanced between the security of conventional society and the primal wildness of the Void. These two opposing forces vie for control of your life and this struggle is seen in the Norn's Thread.

Late Bloomers

I mentioned earlier that short threads can indicate either a late bloomer or an early quitter. Let's look at this a little more closely.

Norn's Threads that begin high in the hand (Figure 8.4) show people whose talents ripen later in life. The advantage to this is that when success finally comes, they are in a better position to enjoy it. You see this on the hands of a lot of people who return to school in their thirties and forties. Confucius said, "Great talents ripen late," and this is definitely true of those with high Norn's Threads.

Sometimes the thread ends before it reaches the fingers (Figure 8.5). It could be said that the path leading to the person's destiny is under construction! Often this is found on people who don't think about the long term and are content to get by from day to day. On the other hand, it can mean that they don't have to worry about their future because it's already taken care of. Maybe they have money saved up or a good retirement plan.

If found with certain other signs (such as the branch of Bragi, which you will find in chapter 9), a thread that ends early can be a sign of great success early in life. The reasoning here is that these people accomplish their life's work while they are young, and then get to play for the rest of their lives! In any case, this type of thread signifies a future that is open to many possibilities. Over time the line may grow longer if the person's attitudes and circumstances change.

Yes, the Thread Can Change!

The Norn's Thread is one of the most volatile features of the hand, often changing within the space of a few weeks. If you keep a "hand diary" and record images of your hand over the course of a year, you will notice the branches and threads of the hand are constantly changing. This is proof that we create our destiny through our will instead of being helpless puppets of fate. So if your thread isn't exactly what you would prefer, it's possible to change the course of your life though applied effort.

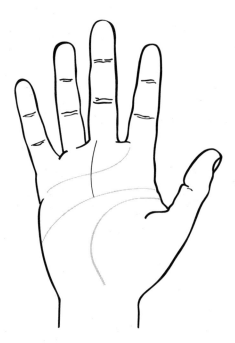

FIGURE 8.4—Norn's Thread
beginning late

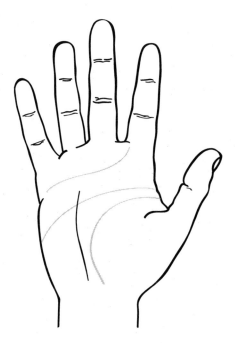

FIGURE 8.5—Norn's Thread
ending early

When Do the Changes Occur?

In a general sense, the Norn's Thread can be used for divination, as it reveals the ages when lifestyle changes are likely to occur along the life path. Where the thread crosses the branch of Mimir is roughly the age of thirty-four, and the branch of Freya is approximately forty-nine. You will notice that the distance from the wrist to the branch of Mimir is considerably longer than any other segment. This shows our formative years—from birth to about age thirty-four.

As the thread weaves its way along the hand, you can tell the approximate ages when personality changes occurred, and sometimes the nature of these changes. Variations in the direction and quality of the thread indicate periods when major lifestyle revisions occurred. Outward breaks toward the heel of the hand (Figure 8.6) indicate a break with tradition, usually found on people who have experienced an epiphany, or spiritual awakening, that affected their life in a positive way. An inward break (Figure 8.7) shows that a person chose to return to past influences. A good example would be a "wild child" who calms down and accepts traditional family values.

Multiple Beginnings

People with three or more beginnings to the thread (Figure 8.8) have experienced many false starts before they finally found their correct life path. These people have tried on many hats before they found one that fit. Their teenage years were spent exploring different identities, social groups, and interests. Usually they will have tried several completely different careers before settling on one that they are happy with.

The interesting thing here is that each beginning shows a separate component of people's personalities. You can actually see the different forces—such as family, society, or the Void—that went into shaping their particular lifestyle by the way the thread veers toward other branches. This is almost as good as looking into their secret diary! Use your powers for good, please.

A double Norn's Thread (Figure 8.9) indicates a person with a double life path. In other words, this person can follow either path to fulfillment and success. The major problem is deciding which path to follow: the conservative

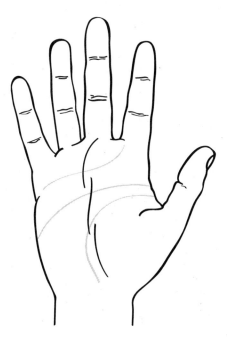

FIGURE 8.6—Inward-breaking
Norn's Thread

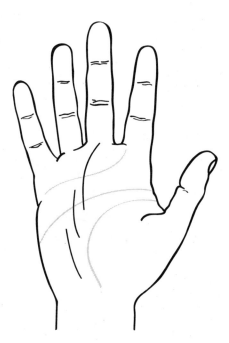

FIGURE 8.7—Outward-breaking
Norn's Thread

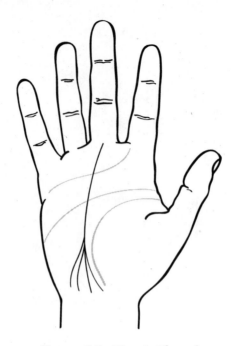

FIGURE 8.8—Norn's Thread
with multiple beginnings

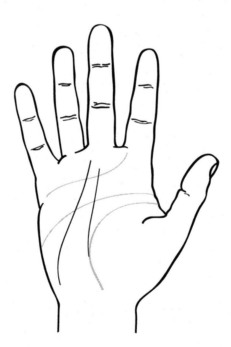

FIGURE 8.9—Double Norn's Thread

path indicated by the thread nearest to the thumb, or the more exploratory path indicated by the thread beginning in or around the Void.

A Word About Free Will

Before we leave the Norn's Threads we should think about an important question. Do we have free will, or are our lives predestined from the moment of our birth? Arguments from both points of view are compelling. Paradoxically, perhaps both are true.

We are a combination of many factors: genetic, environmental, and mystical. Obviously our genes have a great deal to say about who we are. Equally important is the environment in which we're raised. Mystical influences involve such things as karma brought in from past lives.

What makes humans unique in the animal kingdom is that we have very few hard-wired responses. Our nervous system is flexible and adaptable. If you want to see an incredibly intricate hard-wired reaction, look at a spider's web the next time you're walking through the woods. Nobody taught the spider how to create such a breathtakingly beautiful structure; it was born with the required knowledge. Likewise, freshly hatched baby chicks know to run for cover when a predatory bird flies overhead. Psychologists call these innate behaviors *release mechanisms.*

Humans have very few recognized release mechanisms of this type. Rather than being born with complex instinctive reactions, we learn to respond to the world through society's instruction and the ever-popular method of trial and error. We learn to choose from a number of possible reactions and apply the one that fits a particular situation best. In other words, we have free will. Or do we?

A great deal depends on whether or not you believe you have free will. The Roman statesman Seneca remarked dryly, "The Fates lead him who is willing. Those who aren't, they drag." On the other hand, African shamans teach that a person's destiny is fan-shaped, meaning that each direction you may choose to walk leads to a different outcome. As I hinted earlier, perhaps our lives are a combination of both free will and predestiny.

Back to School

Since life on this earth is meant to be a learning experience, isn't it possible that our souls decided before birth what these lessons will be? Perhaps the disappointments, setbacks, and crises we experience are part of the lesson plan we designed for ourselves before we were born. Uncomfortable as they may be at the time, these learning experiences quickly pass and we come out stronger and (we hope!) wiser.

The soul existed before we were born and will continue to exist after we're dead. From this higher perspective our entire lifetime is just a fleeting moment, a momentary discomfort for the soul's benefit. Think of the last time you went to the doctor to get a shot. A quick "Ouch!" and you felt better afterward. Is it too much of a stretch to suppose that we chose the major events in our lives while we were in spirit? Just something to think about.

You Are the Weaver!

Destiny isn't something big and ominous that is written in stone, waiting for us to blindly run into it. Rather, it is flexible; we recreate our personal destiny with each decision we make. It's up to us to listen carefully to the whisperings of our soul. Only then can we make the right decisions and begin to weave the threads of our own destiny!

> *It is best for a person to be middle-wise*
> *Not over-cunning and clever.*
> *No man may know his future*
> *So let him sleep in peace.*
>
> THE WORDS OF THE HIGH ONE

9

OTHER IMPORTANT SIGNS AND PORTENTS

Learned I grew then, wise with knowledge.
Word from the Word gave words to me;
Deeds from the Deed gave deeds to me.

THE WORDS OF THE HIGH ONE

Before moving on to the study of the palm runes, we'll look at a few other important branches and marks of special interest. Some of these signs are fairly common, others very rare. While almost everyone will have the three major branches of Sif, Freya, and Mimir, not everyone will have the branches discussed in this chapter. However, they appear often enough that you should be able to recognize them when you see them.

Branch of Bragi

The *branch of Bragi* looks like a Norn's Thread, except it ends under the finger of Bragi (Figure 9.1). Remember we learned that for a line to be a true Norn's Thread, it must end beneath Hoenir. The

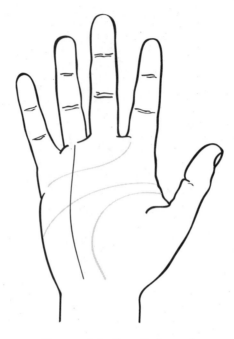

FIGURE 9.1—Bragi's branch

Bragi branch is one of the lines beginning palmists often mistake for the Norn's Thread.

When present, this branch is a good omen. It predicts fame or success in a field related to fashion, entertainment, art, or culture. On the hand of a person aspiring to show business, it's a great sign. Most actors and fashion models show this branch, and I've seen it in the hands of talented musicians. Look to the Norn's Thread to see if this success comes early or late in life.

Branch of Loki

Sometimes called a *line of communication* (or *charisma*), the *branch of Loki* runs along the heel of the hand and ends under the Loki finger (Figure 9.2). When it's clear and unbroken, these people could earn a sizable income from their communication skills alone. Aunt Eliza used to jokingly call it the "b.s." line, because people with the Loki branch can really lay it on thick!

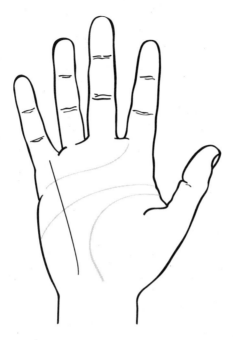

FIGURE 9.2—Loki's branch

The Fylgia

According to the *Poetic Edda,* the *Fylgia* was a guardian spirit assigned by the Norns to people at birth. Today we would probably call this entity a guardian angel or spirit guide. The presence of the Fylgia mark shows the period of protection the guardian provides. The Fylgia mark looks like a second Sif's branch (Figure 9.3). Some people have more than one, showing members of their "soul family" who are looking out for them.

Nanna's Crown

Nanna's Crown can be seen as an arc or bow on the heel of the hand, surrounding the mount of Nanna (Figure 9.4). This special mark shows people with exceptional psychic and emotional sensitivity. They will be talented "people readers," profoundly intuitive and empathic. They will most likely

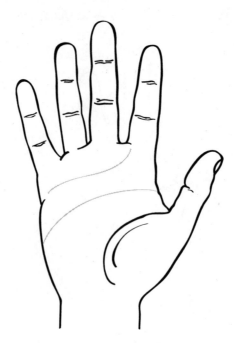

FIGURE 9.3—The Fylgia

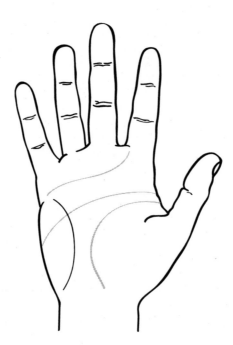

FIGURE 9.4—Nanna's Crown

experience mood swings. Since Nanna was the goddess of the moon, people under her influence will follow the lunar cycles, their energy waxing and waning during a thirty-day period.

The Butterfly

I love to find the sign of the *Butterfly* on a person's palm. It shows a free and playful childlike spirit. These people must be wonderful friends to have around; they just seem to attract good feelings to them all the time. The butterfly is usually found somewhere between Sif's branch and the Norn's Thread (Figure 9.5). It also forms the palmar rune *Daeg* (ᛞ), which we'll examine more closely in the next chapter.

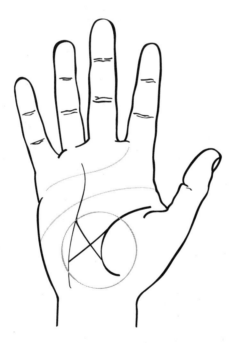

Figure 9.5—Butterfly

The Mystic Cross

The *Mystic Cross,* one of the oldest classical signs of intuition and psychic ability, is found between Freya and Mimir (Figure 9.6). After all, intuition is the bridge between the head and the heart.

If the cross connects Mimir (head) with Freya (heart), then the person will be exceptionally intuitive in both romantic and business affairs. However, if one of the legs of the cross doesn't connect to one of the branches, the person will be blinded in that area. In other words, if the cross is attached to Mimir but not Freya, the person will be able to read people in every aspect of their lives except where the heart is concerned. If the cross is attached to Freya but not Mimir, the person will be successful at human relationships but probably have trouble making the correct intuitive decisions involving work or business.

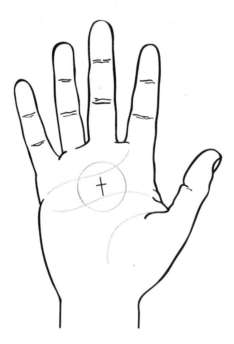

FIGURE 9.6—Mystic Cross

The Crow's Foot

The unusual marking of the *Crow's Foot* (Figure 9.7), which consists of three lines beginning near the wrist and spreading toward the fingers, shows that the person either is a witch or was a witch in a previous life. At any rate, these people will have the ability to "cast spells," so they have to be very careful what they say. If they wish harm on others, it will probably happen! They usually admit that they are a little spooky sometimes, not only to other people, but to themselves as well.

I hope you've enjoyed looking at a few of the markings that can be found in the hand. This chapter is meant to acquaint you with some of the more common signs, but there are a lot more to be found if you're interested. I suggest you find a good book on Chinese palmistry and study it. The Chinese have located and identified literally hundreds of special signs and markings!

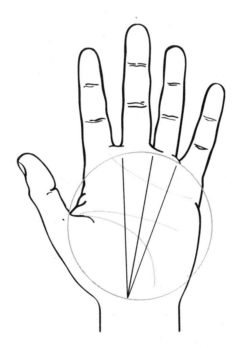

FIGURE 9.7—Crow's Foot

Now it's time to move on to the crux of the runic palmistry system—the palm runes!

The fool thinks that those who laugh at him
Are all his friends
Unaware when he sits with wiser men
How ill they speak of him.

THE WORDS OF THE HIGH ONE

Part II

THE RUNES

. . . know how to carve them; know how to stain them; know how to prove them; know how to evoke them; know how to respect them; know how to read them; know how to send them . . .

THE WORDS OF THE HIGH FATHER

10

An Introduction to the Runes

A man can only attain knowledge with the help of those who possess it. This must be understood from the very beginning. One must learn from him who knows.

George Gurdjieff

Up to now, we've been examining the runes as they appear in the hand. But we must not forget that traditionally, the runes were usually carved on wood or stone and used for divinatory purposes. Now we'll take a few moments to examine the runes in their original form.

The runes are a set of powerful magical symbols which, according to legend, were brought into the world by Odin, the All-Father. You'll recall that Odin sacrificed himself on Yggdrasil in order to obtain the secret key to reading the runes. In the *Elder Edda*, he describes how he won them:

> *Nine whole nights on a wind-rocked tree*
> *Pierced by sharp spear, for nine nights I hung.*

Offered to Odin, myself to myself
On that tree which no man has ever seen.

They gave me no bread, nor quenched my
Thirst with mead. I gazed down, and with a
Loud scream I took up the Runes.
From Yggdrasil I then fell.

Historically, the runes date back to antiquity. As early as the fifth century A.D., runic inscriptions appeared in Britain, but many authorities believe that runes are descended from the very earliest forms of written language. Versions of the runes have been accredited to the Celts, the Druids, the Norse, Germans, and the Anglo-Saxons.

The most common form of runic divination uses a set of symbols known as the *Elder Futhark*, named after the first six letters of the twenty-four–character runic alphabet (*F, U, TH, A, R, K*). However, the use of the runes as an alphabetical system came into practice a long time after the runes originally appeared. Originally each rune was a magical symbol representing a concept or idea, usually indicating a natural force. You'll see what I mean when we get into interpreting the runes.

The runes function on many levels. They serve as symbols of protection, shielding you from negative influences. They also function in a magical sense as casters of spells, bringing luck, love, or wealth to the person who knows how to properly use them. And finally they serve as a means of divination, providing you with glimpses into your life (and the lives of others) through the process of a runecast. We'll approach these various facets of the runes one step at a time and learn how they can help improve our understanding of ourselves and others.

"... Know How to Read Them ..."

The twenty-four runic symbols are traditionally divided into three families (or *aettir*) of eight. The first set is *Freya's Eight*, the second set is *Hagall's Eight*, and the third set is *Tyr's Eight*. Interestingly enough, the three aettir are not named after gods, but after the rune that begins each group of eight. In *Northern Mysteries and Magick,* Freya Aswynn links these aet (eight) with the Norns, but that's another story! Keep in mind that each rune is a symbol for a specific natural force as you read the basic meanings below. (Note: *Reversed,* and the positions of *past, present,* and *future* or *outcome* all refer to a three-rune divination, explained in detail in the next chapter.)

Freya's Eight

Fehu (*FEE-oo*): Originally a symbol for cattle, this rune symbolizes material wealth or gain. In divinatory terms, it means you will gain your desire or achieve your goal. When you see this rune, you must think in terms of acquisition and expansion of assets. It also indicates a major purchase. Reversed, it can indicate that you're about to spend a lot of money that you weren't expecting to, or are about to take a loss. It can also mean that it will be a while before you're paid for the work you're doing now.

Uruz (*OO-rooz*): Symbolic of the wild ox, this means good health, emotional well-being, strong physical stamina, and resistance to negative influences. Uruz literally stands for wild, untamed animal energy. Usually, Uruz predicts that you're going to need every ounce of that energy to deal with a sudden situation. In a relationship, it represents the male of the pair. Reversed, it can mean that you're about to be caught off-guard by a sudden powerful change, so be warned! Reversed in the past position, it means you've already failed to take advantage of the moment, an opportunity was lost, or that you're going to have to spend a great deal of energy cleaning up a mess you made in the past.

Thurisaz (*THUR-a-saz*): A glyph representing both Thor's hammer and a thorn (as in "in your side"), Thurisaz can mean a sudden stroke of good fortune from out of nowhere. Why is it a protective rune? A thorn exists in order to protect the plant. Reversed, it means you have a persistent problem or negative situation you just can't seem to get rid of. Look to other runes for solutions.

Ansuz (*AN-sooz* or *AN-sur*): Literally, an answer—a communication such as advice, news, or the answer to a problem. Of course, the presence of an answer implies the existence of a question, doesn't it? The important thing here is to be clear about the question, otherwise the answer won't make sense. Ansuz often shows the need to seek advice from a wiser head. Reversed, it indicates lies and deception. Always get a second opinion, or check out the facts whenever Ansuz appears reversed.

Raidho (*RAY-tho*): Implies travel. Upright, it is a journey for pleasure or personal gain. Reversed, it can mean a trip on an unpleasant errand or complications preventing a planned pleasure trip. On a more esoteric level, the journey referred to is on the spiritual plain, so it can mean advancement in a goal if upright, or delays in a goal if reversed.

Ken (*ken*): Representing knowledge and attitude, Ken tells us that we need to fully understand our situation before making a decision. Often it predicts a sudden flash of insight or prescience. Reversed, it means we're about to plunge into dangerous waters without knowing what we're doing. Get more information! Reversed in the past position, it can mean that it's too late to correct a thoughtless mistake.

Gifu (*GIFF-oo*): Literally, a gift. This can be a material gift from a loved one, but more often means an extremely useful piece of advice or information that is bestowed upon you by someone else. Gifu also refers to your natural talents and abilities which may be about to emerge for the first time. It also means "gifts from above," as in nice things that happen to you from out of the blue. This rune is always positive, as it looks the same reversed as right side up!

Wunjo (*WUN-yo*): Another positive rune, this predicts success and happiness. Think "joy"! Things just seem to become easier for a while. The wind is about to blow your way for a while, so enjoy it. Reversed, it means the opposite: Prepare yourself for difficult times—but they'll pass.

Hagall's Eight

Hagall (*HAY-goll*): Meaning "hail," Hagall represents forces out of your control that cause changes. These can lead to delays and setbacks, but they could also be beneficial changes that happen to come at an inconvenient time. Hagall is another rune that has the same meaning reversed: Expect the unexpected.

Neid (*rhymes with "hide"*): This rune represents imposed restrictions and limitations, delays, frustrations; obstacles standing between you and your goal; strong desires that remain unsatisfied; a time spent learning difficult lessons; building strength of character through practicing patience; deferred rewards. Neid is not one of the happier runes, but these barriers can be dealt with through patience and perseverance. Necessity is the mother of invention. Give it time.

Is (*ice*): From the Norse word for ice, this literally indicates a frozen moment. Like ducks stuck to a frozen lake, you're going to be here for a while. Imagine trying to drive up an icy hill; you rev the motor and the wheels spin, but you get nowhere. This is a feeling many of us know all too well. The only good news here is that it will pass. You must learn to live with the situation until your chance for advancement comes up. Often Is advises a voluntary cessation of current activities until a more auspicious time offers itself.

Jera (*YER-ah*): Suggesting a cycle of planting, growing, and harvesting, Jera advises you to enjoy the fruits of your efforts. This rune reminds us that all things come in due time, and not a moment sooner or later than they are supposed to. Jera suggests that it's time to take care of loose ends, settle old debts, and put closure to any unfinished business. Modern rune magicians also associate Jera with a positive outcome to legal situations. The lesson is that things happen in their proper time, and sometimes you must wait for the fruit to ripen before picking it. In the outcome position, it means that your time has arrived!

Yr (*ear*): A powerful rune of protection. When Yr turns up, it signifies that your goals are attainable and realistic. Very positive outcome!

Perdhro (*PERTH-ro*): Some authorities think this symbol represents a dice cup, such as is used in games of chance. Literally, *Perdhro* means "rolling the dice." A secret is about to be revealed; something that was previously a mystery is about to be brought to light. You may not know everything at this time, but you will find out when you need to. Lost objects will be found. Someone is about to spill the beans. It can also portend a recovery of health, an advancement where there was delay, or an unexpected benefit resulting from an action in the past. Depending on the context of the question, it can also mean a sudden unearned monetary gain. Reversed, it can mean disappointment and loss. If this comes up reversed, be wary about loaning money to a friend—you may lose both.

Eolh (*EE-ol*): Probably the most versatile overall symbol of protection, Eolh predicts positive influences entering your life. Remember the peace sign from the sixties? Often these beneficial influences come from friends and loved ones. Reversed, it can mean a period of vulnerability where you are more likely to be hurt both physically and emotionally.

Sig (*sig*): Another powerful rune of protection, Sig assures victory. Like a bolt of lightning, it gives you the power necessary to overcome obstacles and achieve goals. Sig is an extremely powerful rune whose force is sometimes overwhelming. It has no reversed meaning; it's always positive.

Tyr's Eight

Tyr (*tur*): Another rune signifying victory. Usually this victory is associated with a competition of some kind. This can be anything from an athletic event to winning a sales contract. It gives you the steadfastness, motivation, and courage to fight for what's yours and win it. Reversed, it can indicate a lack of motivation, despondency, or depression that generates failure and self-defeating behaviors.

Beorc (*BEE-york*): In an upright position, Beorc predicts a joyful event within the family. Reversed, it warns of domestic problems. Beorc also deals with the birth of ideas and projects nearest to the heart. Think in terms of expansion—both of your family (including friends) and of your creativity.

Ehwaz (*AY-waz*): This usually indicates a positive change involving travel. In a material sense, it can mean a job opportunity requiring relocation. In the spiritual sense, it suggests moving to a different level of enlightenment. At any rate, it means you're moving in the right direction and should continue. Oddly, the reversed meaning isn't necessarily negative. Reversed, Ehwaz can indicate a short journey for pleasure.

Manaz (*MON-ahz*): As the rune of service to humanity, this indicates that you can count on help from those around you. Manaz reminds you that your associations with others are important. The key word here is *interdependence*—working with others to achieve a desired result. It also suggests a need to be of service to others, often indicating a person with strong humanitarian instincts. Reversed, it can show a self-centered, selfish attitude, or that you're going to have to deal with your problems all by yourself for the time being.

Lagu (*LAW-goo*): Signifies intuition and instincts. When upright, Lagu means that you're about to enter a situation you're well suited for. The word *lagu* means "lake," so if you go with the flow, all will be well. Reversed, it can mean you're in a situation that you're not well suited for. You're swimming against the tide and it will eventually wear you out. You made a bad judgment against your better instincts, and now you're in over your head. Yow!

 Ing (*eeng*): Almost always positive, this rune indicates a sense of relief and satisfaction after successfully completing a task. All the work is done; now it's time to relax and take pride in what you've accomplished.

Daeg (*DAY-egg*): This rune means a new beginning; positive changes occurring slow and steady over time; letting go of the past and looking forward to the new day. It also means the light of day is going to shine on something formerly hidden in darkness. In other words, something hidden from you will be revealed.

Othel (*OH-thel*): This symbol is associated with inheritance, but doesn't always mean that. Upright, it indicates an increase in material possessions, usually through the help of friends or family. Reversed, it can warn of a decrease in material possessions. Not necessarily a loss, you may just decide to sell off all your old junk!

Odin's Rune

Wyrd (*weird*): A relatively modern addition to the Futhark, this symbol is represented by a blank rune. This means that the outcome is not meant for you to know; you just have to accept things as they are. Remember, the Wyrd were the three Norn sisters, so this rune means that the outcome (your fate) is entirely out of your hands. Wyrd urges you to trust in your higher power and accept whatever happens. It's a frustrating rune to draw when you want an immediate answer to your question, but what can you do? Sometimes you have to proceed on trust alone.

"... Know How to Carve Them ..."

Now that you know what the runes mean, you need to obtain a set and learn to do readings. Although many excellent sets of runes are commercially available, I strongly urge you to make your own if you're serious about learning to use them. When you make them yourself, they become charged with your particular energy. My first set was obtained at a bookstore, but after a while I retired them and made my own. They just seem to work better.

The runes should be carved on small wooden plaques or tiles on the first day of the New Moon. Oak or ash are the preferred woods. I made mine from ash in honor of the world tree Yggdrasil. Since you will be making twenty-five of them (one is left blank), they should be small enough to fit inside a drawstring bag. 1″ x ¾″ is a convenient size if you choose to make them in tile form. A readily available source of ashwood, by the way, is a baseball bat!

Choosing the wood is important. I made my set from a freshly fallen limb. Cutting cross-sections from the limb made excellent round disks for my runes. I allowed the wood to dry and polished the disks with emory cloth until the surfaces were smooth.

On the day of the New Moon, I carefully carved the symbols on each disk. I cheated a little and used an engraving tool. Be sure to wear proper protective equipment when you do this! If you're skilled at woodcarving, you may prefer to use hammer and chisel, or sear them in with a woodburning tool. Just be careful.

I don't recommend that you finish the runes with lacquer or varnish. Probably a little wax would be okay. You really don't want anything to come between you and the runes; your energies must be able to freely mingle with that of the wood.

Some early sets of runes were carved in bone. It seems to me that these runes would tend to take on the energies of the animal from which they came. I personally wouldn't make a set from animal bones unless I knew that the animal had died of natural causes. However, if you have a favorite animal totem, it's just possible that a set of runes made from its bones would be immensely powerful.

"... Know How to Stain Them ..."

To add color and contrast to the carved runes, I suggest you use a natural pigment such as walnut. Apply the pigment with an artist's brush and allow it to dry. You may want to apply several coats to make the symbols really stand out. I also stain the reverse side of my runes to eradicate any telltale markings that would distinguish one rune from the other while facedown. Some rune magicians insist that the symbols should be stained in with blood—but you didn't hear this from me!

"... Know How to Respect Them ..."

Never loan your runes to another person! In a very real sense they are you, and if you give them to someone else it's the same as trusting them with your well-being. Always keep the runes in a clean leather or cotton drawstring bag, and handle them with proper respect and reverence. Remember, they are powerful.

If you give readings to other people, a small amount of their energy will be absorbed by your runes. This is good. It enables you and your client to establish a bond of communication that will help trigger your natural clairvoyant senses. For this reason I try not to do too many rune readings in a single day; the energies can become muddled. Usually these borrowed energies are faint enough to dissipate after a few hours, so your runes will be "clean" by the next day. You may want to make two sets of runes, one for your personal use and the other for giving readings to other people.

Now that you know a little bit about the runes, in the next chapter we'll learn more about how to use these ancient symbols of power to give readings and cast spells.

The mind alone knows what lies near the heart,
Each must be his own judge.
The worst affliction for a wise man
Is to yearn for what he cannot enjoy.

THE WORDS OF THE HIGH ONE

11

RUNE MAGICK

From the Runes of the Giants, and from the Runes of the Gods, I can read the Truth. I have wandered through all nine worlds, and also through Hel itself...

THE LAY OF VAFTHRUDNIR

Now that we've learned the basic meaning of the runes, we'll take a look at how to do a simple reading with the runestones. Then, in the following chapter we'll learn how to integrate the runecast with a runic palmistry reading.

"... Know How to Prove Them ..."

After much internal debate, I decided against describing all the myriad ways to perform a runecast. To do so would have made this book twice as large as it is. There are already many excellent books on this topic and I would only repeat what has already been written. See the Bibliography at the back of this book for a few recommended sources of information on rune layouts. I will, however, describe a couple of simple divination techniques to get you started.

One Rune Method

This method is called a *One Rune Draw*. It's a great way to determine the overall tone of your day.

Mix your runes either in their bag or in a bowl. Now, without peeking, select a rune. This rune will tell you how your day is going to go. If you draw one of the beneficial runes (Sig or Eolh), well and good! However, if you draw one of the negative runes (such as Neid or Is), your day will have complications. However, since forewarned is forearmed, the runes help you prepare for these obstacles. At least you won't be caught by surprise.

Simple as it is, the one rune method is a surprisingly effective technique. It also prepares you for the *Three Rune Draw*.

Three Rune Method

Once you're comfortable with the One Rune Draw, try this. Select three runes, just as you did earlier with one rune, and lay them in a row in the order you drew them. The first rune represents your past. This will tell you what situations, decisions, or talents have influenced your current situation. The middle rune is your present, and will give you a general picture of where you are at the moment. The third rune is your future or outcome. It will tell you how your current situation will turn out if you keep going in the direction you're headed.

What if the outcome rune is bad? Oh no! Actually, we know that our futures are flexible, changing with each decision we make. If the third rune predicts a bad outcome, ask yourself what you can do to change it. Sometimes the three runes on the table suggest solutions to your problems. If you're at wit's end trying to come up with an answer, try this: Concentrate on your question and draw a fourth rune. This rune will tell you what powers, strategies, or talents you can call upon to better your situation.

For example, I just did a rune layout for the question "Will this book be successful?" The three runes I drew were Raidho (reversed), Manaz, and Fehu (reversed).

Raidho reversed in the past position indicates a lack of movement in the past—procrastination, delays, and so on. This is certainly right on the money. I put off writing this book for years until I felt the time was right. Now I wish I had started it five years ago when the idea first hit me! Moving to the present position, we encounter Manaz right side up. This indicates that my work is intended to help others (and it is!) and that it will have value to those who read it. Good news so far. But now we come upon Fehu reversed in the future position! Oh no! Doesn't this mean that there will be a delay or lack of progress? Don't panic. Let's draw a fourth rune and see how to avert (or deal with) this ill omen.

Ah good! The fourth rune is Beorc right side up (ᛒ). In this sense it means the birth of a creative project or idea. So this book will be ultimately successful, but only after a period of frustrating delays and setbacks. Oh well—I can live with that! If I had drawn Hagall, Is, or Neid, I could look forward to endless delays, disappointments, and heartache.

I hope this gives you a good idea of how runecasts can help you answer life's more difficult questions. Practice this method for a few weeks before trying it out on others.

Reading for Others

To give readings to others using the Three Rune Method, ask them to reach into the bag and hand you any three runes, which you place in a row. An alternate method of selection (which I prefer) is to scatter all the runes face down on the table. When using this method for others, ask them to mix the runes around, taking care not to turn them over. If a rune accidentally turns over or falls off the table, this is considered a choice, so you use the rune in the reading. After they're through mixing, I ask them to pass their hands over the runes and to select one they feel "drawn" toward. Sometimes it seems to feel warm, or perhaps it calls out to be selected. Oddly enough, even people who have never had a reading before understand what is expected. Continue the process until three runes have been chosen.

Place the three selected runes in a row (just as you did before) and interpret the past, present, and the probable outcome of the situation in question. If they're heading for trouble have them draw a fourth rune to obtain advice on how to best deal with the problem. Sometimes it may be necessary to call upon the rune itself for magickal protection. We'll learn how to do this next.

"... Know How to Evoke Them ..."

One of the most powerful functions of the runes is their use as protective talismans. By wearing a particular rune on your person you evoke the natural forces it represents. These forces provide an added layer of protection against hostile energies. The magickal power of each rune follows.

Freya's Eight

 Fehu (*FEE-oo*): Useful for bringing matters to a head or removing a tedious delay. Helps create a positive outcome to events. Protects against the ill wishes of others who are hostile.

 Uruz (*OO-rooz*): Use for good health and emotional well-being. Attracts new possibilities into your life. Helps you adapt to a sudden change.

 Thurisaz (*THUR-a-saz*): General protection from the unknown. Provides psychic and physical shielding from hostile forces. It is the power of faith manifested. Provides the strength to shrug off negative events.

Ansuz (*AN-sooz* or *AN-sur*): Enhances creative and communication energies. Provides help during an exam or test. Hastens a response to an unanswered question. Good to have with you on a job interview!

Raidho (*RAY-tho*): Provides protection on journeys—both physical and spiritual. Helps keep matters moving along quickly; prevents delays and obstacles.

Ken (*ken*): Enhances creative energies and provides insights and mental clarity. Helps you obtain flashes of intuitive insights when you need them the most. Ken is associated with fire, and in this role it can help fan the flame of sexual attraction between two lovers.

Gifu (*GIFF-oo*): Use to attract positive events into your life. Also use to increase the chances of receiving presents, monetary or material gains, or information that you can parlay into a profitable endeavor. Gifu is a powerful summoning rune, and can help you evoke hidden talents and reveal latent potentials.

Wunjo (*WUN-yo*): Use for success in all endeavors. Use as a lucky charm when you want to better your odds of success. Helps align the universal forces in your favor. Makes a thing easier than it normally would have been.

Hagall's Eight

Hagall (*HAY-goll*): Use for spiritual development, life lessons, insights, and wisdom. Gives luck in a bad situation. Hard times will get better. Helps your intuition forewarn you before danger strikes.

Neid (*rhymes with "hide"*): Use to fulfill desires. Ends loneliness or dissatisfaction. Helps obsessive/compulsive behavior and addictions. Use to help the universe furnish what you need. (Note: There's a big difference between what you want and what you need!)

Is (*ice*): Cools off a situation. Brings action to a halt. Keeps things as they are (freezes them). Slows down changes. Useful in curbing impatience. Helps cool off a hot temper. Preserves a situation in its present form.

Jera (*YER-ah*): Use for fertility, rewards for effort, and positive outcomes to legal matters. Promotes cycle of work and reward. Promotes fertility and helps launch new projects.

Yr (*ear*): A powerful rune of protection. Use it to banish harmful forces and to clear the air of negative emotions. Heals grudges and removes obstacles. Helps empaths throw off the negative emotions they absorb from others.

Perdhro (*PERTH-ro*): Use for self-improvement, enlightenment, and development of psychic abilities. Helpful for finding out hidden knowledge and learning secrets. Helpful for obtaining occult knowledge.

Eolh (*EE-ol*): Probably the most versatile overall symbol of protection. Notice that it reaches its arms to heaven, calling down the power from above to provide protection and safety to the user. Use during periods of vulnerability to strengthen your defenses. Eolh brings peace and tranquility into your life.

Sig (*sig*): Another powerful rune of protection, Sig endows self-confidence, personal power, and increases charisma and assurance. A very aggressive rune, the Sig energy is a bit hard to control. If you find yourself overwhelmed by its impact (or becoming too cocky), switch to Eolh.

Tyr's Eight

Tyr (*tur*): Use this warrior rune for strength and aggression. Once was used to evoke more power during combat. Warriors used to carve it on their weapons before entering combat. Use it to increase your competitive edge! Also good when you need to tough something out. Helps ensure victory.

 Beorc (*BEE-york*): A protection rune for family, friends, and household. It's good as a talisman to protect children. I've etched it on my pets' tags to help protect them from injury or accident.

Ehwaz (*AY-waz*): Evokes a blessing on a sudden change, such as a new house, job, or journey. Helps ease the adjustment period, and increases your adaptability and resourcefulness.

Manaz (*MON-ahz*): The rune of service to mankind, this is useful during those troubling times when you think you're all alone. It evokes the tribal force and lets you know that you're not as alone as you think—others are watching out for you! If you're a student in need of a teacher, Manaz will help you attract one. If you're a stranger in search of a friend, you can count on finding one.

 Lagu (*LAW-goo*): Enhances sensitivity, empathy, intuition, and earth energies. If you're trying to develop your psychic abilities or to take them to the next level, this rune will help you.

Ing (*eeng*): A symbol literally signifying the male genitals, this rune is useful to promote fertility, generate positive creative energies, and successfully complete a task or project.

 Daeg (*DAY-egg*): Helps usher in a new beginning, the dawn of a new day. Old situations and strategies are let go to make room for a fresh start. Useful in breaking a bad habit.

Othel (*OH-thel*): Use to protect money and material possessions. A good rune to have around the house or automobile.

Odin's Rune

Wyrd (*weird*): While it may seem odd (or weird) to carry around a blank amulet, remember that you're evoking the forces of nature by concentrating your mind in a certain direction. Odin shows that you're willing to turn your life over to the will of God; you're asking for total acceptance of your fate. Wyrd gives you the strength and resourcefulness to accept the outcome no matter what.

"... Know How to Send Them ..."

Not only can you summon rune magick for your own uses, it can also be sent out to others to help them make changes in their lives. But be very, very careful. Casting spells is a tricky and often hazardous business. The laws of karma assure that whatever you send out invariably comes back to you, so make sure the runic spells you cast out are positive ones. Do not be tempted to use runic magick for personal gain or for revenge; folklore is chock full of stories about the awful consequences of magick misused. Always act out of love and compassion.

If you wish to use runic magick to help another, select the appropriate rune and hold it in your hand. Make your mind as peaceful and serene as you can, and imagine that person's face in front of you. Really focus in on them; experience all the feelings they inspire in you. When you feel that you are in spiritual contact with them, send them the protective energies of the rune's magick with all your strength. The rest is in the hands of your higher power.

If necessary, make them an amulet to carry around with the appropriate rune drawn on it. I draw these with gold ink on small pieces of wood or stone. I always do this with runes found in the palm, which we'll look at in the next chapter. Some people will have their protective rune engraved on a medallion by a jeweler. I've also seen protective amulets at New Age stores cast in pewter or silver, and these look very nice.

That's it. This is enough information to get you started on runecasts, and if you want to know more, I suggest you obtain the books recommended in the Bibliography. Refer to the handy crib sheet in the Appendix to help you remember the runes and their meanings. Next we'll look at the final piece in the runic palmistry system: the palm runes!

Nobody is the ruler of his riches or his health,
Although he may often be happy
Ill-luck can strike when least expected.
No-one can command his peace.

THE SUN SONG,
AN ANCIENT NORSE POEM

12

THE MAJOR AND MINOR RUNES OF THE PALM

All true language
is incomprehensible,
Like the chatter
of a beggar's teeth.

ANTONIN ARTAUD

As you will recall, it was my Aunt Eliza who discovered that runes could be found in the palm of the hand. Actually, you'll see that runic symbols appear all around us, including in the limbs of trees, architecture, and road signs. That these runes of power also appear on our bodies should come as no surprise.

It takes a little practice to locate these runic symbols. Once you're familiar with them, though, they seem to leap out at you. The clarity of the runes will differ from hand to hand. Some hands (such as Heimdall types) will have a myriad of lines, making the runes difficult to isolate. Making an ink print of the hand will bring these out more clearly.

Palmists believe that when a line or feature in the hand stands out from the rest, that particular area of the person's life is active.

When active, the branches will be of a flushed or reddish color, and the mounts will be full and prominent. These prominent branches and mounts will indicate the major issues at the present time in the person's life. Therefore, if runes are faint or hidden, it means that the power of the rune is dormant but always ready to help when needed. If the rune stands out prominently, it means that its protective energy has been summoned.

Sometimes it's useful to outline palmar runes with a water-soluble pen to help people see them better. If you work from a print, it's a simple matter to trace the symbols with a highlighter. I usually lay out a set of runes on the table. As I locate the palmar runes, I'll pick up the matching rune and lay it next to the one in their hand. You should see the look on people's faces when they realize they have these awesome symbols of magickal power right in the palm of their hands!

Runes on the Subdominant Hand

Since the subdominant hand represents the person's potential, any runes appearing there are considered hidden or latent abilities. It's important to check to see if these talents have carried over to the dominant hand, which represents the person at the present time. Don't overlook the runes in the subdominant hand. Quite often, these undeveloped abilities will provide the missing pieces to the person's quest for self-fulfillment.

Location, Location, Location!

Where each palm rune appears affects its meaning. The major runes are constructed from the major branches, while the minor runes are usually found in other parts of the hand. Remember that the runes must stand out clearly for maximum effectiveness. If the branches forming the runes are frayed, warped, or have a million tiny twigs shooting off of them, their power will be significantly diminished.

The Major Runes

The major runes are those that are actually constructed from the major branches. Later on, we will examine the minor runes, which are smaller and usually appear under one of the fingers, between branches, or on a mount.

Ehwaz (ᛗ)

Ehwaz is constructed from the branches of Freya, Mimir, Sif, and a Norn's Thread (Figure 12.1). It's a very good omen, for as you'll recall this rune promotes successful changes. Since it contains all the major branches, this success follows people in every aspect of their life. Ehwaz symbolizes evolution, so these people will continually change, evolve, and grow all their days. They will have a gift for starting projects that take off into successful ventures. Ehwaz will add a spontaneous, impulsive, and instinctive element to their behavior; they will act quickly and correctly.

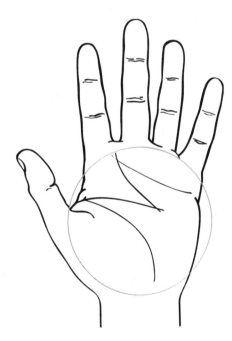

FIGURE 12.1—Ehwaz

Manaz (ᛗ)

Be very careful not to confuse this with Ehwaz (ᛗ) or Daeg (ᛞ)! Manaz is the rune that represents humanity as a whole. People with this rune in their palm (Figure 12.2) will be driven by their humanitarian urges. They will be happiest only when they are helping others. The sign of an old soul, Manaz will put people in touch with the souls of others. Even as children these people will be serious, wise, and mature beyond their years. My grandmother used to say this sign was "*M* for Magician, or *W* for Witch—depending on how they tied you to the stake way back when!" She said it indicated people who, in past lives, were masters of magick or witchcraft. These people will bring these talents into their current life and often are very interested in the occult and metaphysics.

Daeg (ᛞ)

Daeg will occur only if Sif's branch is either short or broken (Figure 12.3). This is a wonderful sign, as these people will be blessed with a positive outlook, an overall sense of happiness, and a childlike freedom of self-expression. Daeg resembles the Butterfly (chapter 9), and has all the same characteristics. These people will be young at heart and love to play.

Ken (ᚲ)

Consisting of the branches of both Frey and Sif (Figure 12.4), Ken will combine the logic of the head with the vitality of life force to forge a powerful combination! These people will possess a keen intellect coupled with an uncanny ability to figure out what's really going on. Very few people will be able to pull the wool over their eyes. These will be the shrewdest people in the world; they are natural players and movers and shakers.

Eolh (ᛉ)

As you will recall, Eolh (Figure 12.5) is the most versatile symbol of overall protection. People fortunate enough to possess this sign will have a charmed life.

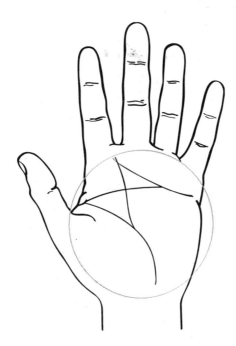

FIGURE 12.2—Manaz

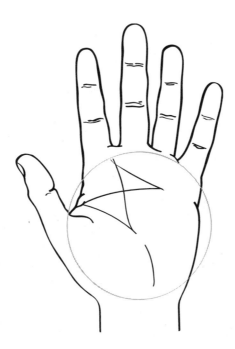

FIGURE 12.3—Daeg

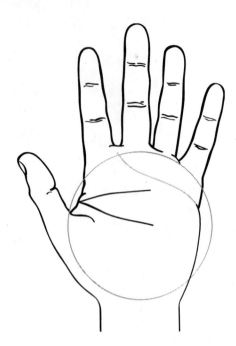

FIGURE 12.4—Ken

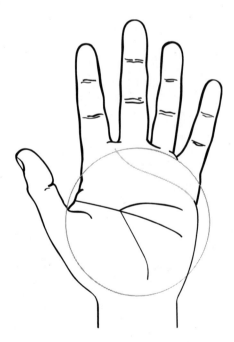

FIGURE 12.5—Eolh

How potent is this sign? I can't promise you anything, but this anecdote will explain why I value this rune so highly I never leave home without it:

One night I was driving home from a company party, where I had been reading palms all night. When I got in my car, sleepy and tired, I noticed a twig lying on the ground in front of my car door. The twig formed a perfect Eolh. Recognizing an omen when I see one, I picked the twig up and placed it on my dashboard.

I had a long drive ahead of me (about two hours or so) and the weather was bad—a mixture of sleet and ice. After a few miles on the highway, my car went into a spin and I glided off onto the shoulder of the road—just in time to avoid an out-of-control sixteen-wheeler that would have ground both me and my car into atoms! That truck literally cleared my front bumper by inches. I was unharmed, if a little shaken. Sometimes magick just happens, and when it does, you don't question it. You'd better believe the twig hangs from my rearview mirror to this day!

Many times Eolh appears at the end of one of the major branches (Figure 12.6). This concentrates Eolh's gentle protective power into one aspect of people's lives.

- If Eolh appears at the end of Sif, it provides physical protection. You will have vast reserves of vitality, enjoy overall good health, and when you do get sick, you'll show amazing recuperative powers.

- If found at the end of Freya, this shows good fortune in the area of romance. Although you may experience some rocky times, eventually you will find the love of your life and spend the rest of it with that person.

- If found at the end of Mimir, Eolh gives the ability to generate new and exciting ideas that will lead to great success. Often these ideas are so radically different, they take time to catch on. You are usually optimistic, with a good attitude and a philosophical approach to life. Your ideas are solid gold!

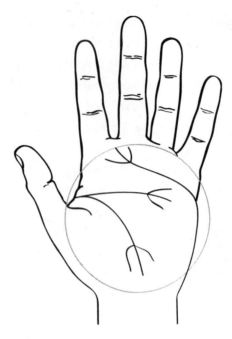

FIGURE 12.6—Eolh at the end of
major branches

The Minor Runes

While the major runes are found in the major branches, the minor runes are usually found in other parts of the hand. Usually they will appear between branches or on the mounts. Imagine that each mount is a storehouse of energy. Each mount has a specific kind of energy (for example, Odin is leadership, Bragi is creative, etc.). The rune appearing on the mount modifies that energy in specific ways. Read on.

Freya's Eight

(Note: The discussion of Ken is found under "The Major Runes" on page 150.)

Fehu: It is a good omen whenever Fehu is found in the hand. If it's under one of the fingers, it presages a positive development in that area of life. If found on one of the mounts, the same rules apply. Fehu enhances the energy of the mount, predicting a successful development in that area.

Fehu is a controlled, graceful energy that manifests itself over a long period of time. Therefore it is the element of craftspeople, people who cultivate their talents. What these talents are will be revealed according to the finger (or upon which mount) it appears.

- If found under Odin, you will succeed in gaining independence from repressive situations or flourish under positions of leadership.

- If found under Hoenir, you could be an excellent philosopher, teacher, or psychologist.

- If found under Bragi, your greatest chance for success and happiness lie in creative positions—artist, writer, designer, architect or engineer, fashion consultant, or even a position in the theater!

- If found under Loki, you have the potential to take advantage of your communication skills and resourcefulness to obtain desired goals. You have the gift of gab and should develop it to its maximum potential.

Fehu will protect you from attack against your vulnerable points, depending on the location of the rune. If found under Odin, for example, your self-esteem will be fortified. If found under Bragi, your creative powers will hold up against a challenge, and so on. You get the picture.

Uruz: Representing a kind of wild, untamed energy like the wild ox it was meant to depict, Uruz teaches how to improve your health and emotional well-being. When found under a finger, it shows the area where you need to concentrate your efforts.

- If found under Odin, the wild Uruz energy fuels the leadership and ego energies. You will be naturally aggressive in a positive way, and would be a good role model for children such as a coach, camp counselor, or club leader.

- If found under Hoenir, it provides protection against temptation. When reversed under Hoenir, it can mean you're worrying too much about a new possibility or choice and should probably just go ahead and do it.

- If found under Bragi, it can lend a wildness to the creative energies. Imagine artists caught up and swept away by their work and you'll get the idea. In this case, the idea controls you, not the other way around.

- If found under Loki, avoid a tendency to brag, make rash promises, or commit yourself beyond your means.

- If found on the mount of Sif, it means that your passionate nature can be overwhelmingly powerful, at times overriding your common sense. When you enter a new relationship, be careful not to be so swept away by the power of your physical attraction that you neglect the emotional and mental aspects of it. In a divinatory sense, it can mean that a new relationship will change your life forever, or an existing relationship will change for the better!

Uruz also helps you adjust to a sudden change in the area indicated. If you have a demanding new job or a tough test in school, you will find protection.

 Thurisaz: Symbolic of Thor, lord of thunder, Thurisaz provides aggressive protective energy to the location where it lies. Thurisaz is action, not thought, so its message is "Go for it!"

You will probably never find this rune under a finger or standing alone on a mount. Thurisaz is almost always seen as a triangle growing from a particular branch. Like a thorn growing on a plant, it provides protection to the area governed by the branch.

- If found on Sif's branch, it shows a period where your physical safety was endangered but you escaped—a near miss, if you will.

- If found on Freya's branch, it shows a heartbreak that has healed.

- If found on Mimir's branch, it can indicate a time when you improved your mind through conscious self-improvement.

If found anywhere on the hand, you are fortunate. You will be protected from psychic attacks if this sign appears anywhere in your hand. No one will be able to cast negative spells your way; Thor will scare them away with his mighty hammer. Thurisaz will give you unshakable self-assurance when you need it most.

 Ansuz: Indicates an answer is forthcoming in the area indicated. The presence of an answer suggests that there must be a question, so it's important to find out what the question is first.

- If found under Odin, it can indicate a talent for answering questions. Usually this means that you give excellent practical advice. Whether or not you follow your own good advice is another question!

- If found under Hoenir, you seek answers to the tough questions: "What is the meaning of life?", "Why are we here?", and so on. Your life is a quest to unravel the mysteries of the universe. Whether you ever receive answers or not doesn't matter—it's the search for the truth that intrigues you.

- If found under Bragi, you will push your creative field to new limits. You will be "on the edge," always seeking new vehicles for self-expression.

- If found under Loki, Ansuz can indicate an unquenchable curiosity about other people. You will be fascinated by the inner workings of people's minds, what motivates them, and why they do the things they do. You will play endless mind games—more with yourself than with others—and have a tendency to create mischief just to see how people will react to it.

If found anywhere on the hand, Ansuz shows a curiosity about the world and an inquiring nature. You will know the correct line of inquiry to obtain the information you require.

 Raidho: Frankly, I've never found this on anyone's palm, but if I do, I'll know it signifies movement in the direction indicated.

- If found under Odin, it shows you're a climber, someone who has your eye on the position just above you.

- If found under Hoenir, you will probably change religions and philosophies many times during your lifetime, gradually moving toward a self-created spirituality.

- If found under Bragi, you're a renaissance person. Multitalented in a variety of creative areas, you will be a jack of all trades (but a master of none). You won't stick with a subject long enough to master it, but will move on to something more intriguing.

- If found under Loki, it means you will gravitate toward a career involving ideas—newspaper, television, radio, writing, sales, or teaching.

Gifu: When found under one of the fingers, it indicates an extraordinary gift in that area. This applies wherever Gifu is found.

 Wunjo: This shows exceptional luck in the area indicated.

Hagall's Eight

(Note: The discussion of Eolh is found under "The Major Runes" on page 150.)

 Hagall: This indicates a blockage. Probable obstacles, out of your control, are preventing the expression of the energy in the area indicated. Removing this obstacle is essential for the energy of the restricted area to manifest itself. Hagall usually indicates an undeveloped or suppressed talent in the area wherein it lies.

Neid: This shows dissatisfaction and frustrated desires in the area indicated. Basically, there is a longing to express the energies of the affected area. In order to be happy, you must turn your longings into reality.

- When found under any of the fingers, it reveals an instinctive (or subconscious) desire for improvement in that area.

- When found near Freya's branch, it shows you have an unrequited love or an unsatisfied emotional need.

- When found on Mimir's branch, you long for intellectual stimulation.

- When found on Sif, you yearn for freedom of movement. Perhaps you wish to improve your physical condition or just want to make an overall improvement in your lifestyle.

Is: This indicates complete blockage of the energy where Is is found. The talent or trait is frozen and can't be manifested at this time. You must learn to unthaw the energy and allow it to flow freely. Often, all you have to do is give yourself permission to do so.

Jera: Shows that your time is near; the talent represented by the area in which Jera is found is about to ripen. A good sign wherever found, it means the waiting may be over. You are about to reap rewards for past work. It can also indicate a cyclic talent, one that waxes and wanes. A lot of creative people have a productive cycle followed by a period of rest. Jera shows this trait.

Yr: This is a powerful rune of protection. It eliminates obstacles and setbacks in the area indicated. It is a good sign to go ahead and venture into the area represented. Yr protects you from the ill wishes of competitors or others who are jealous.

Perdhro: This indicates self-improvement, enlightenment, and developing psychic abilities. You will find out hidden knowledge and learn secrets.

- If found under Odin, it reveals an investigative nature. You will be good at finding things out. Think of detectives, policemen, investigators, or journalists.

- If found under Hoenir, you will have occult talents. You are a mystic, in tune with the secrets of the universe.

- If found under Bragi, you will have creative ways to find out what you wish to know.

- If found under Loki, you will love gossip and personal confidences.

Sig: One of the more aggressive runes, Sig's power is extremely strong. Wherever it appears, you will be wired for 220 volts instead of the usual 110!

- If found under Odin, it gives you so much personal power you have to be careful not to overwhelm the people around you. You can be incredibly direct and single-minded when focused on a goal. Think visionaries and hyperachievers.

- If found under Hoenir, you will have an exceptional sense of personal responsibility. Often you will devote yourself to a cause—protecting animals, human rights, doing missionary work, or volunteering your talents to worthy causes.

- If found under Bragi, your creativity will be almost obsessive in its intensity. When seized by inspiration, you will do without food or sleep until the work is finished. Then you'll probably crash for about a week! Creative intensity is the keyword here.

- If found under Loki, you will simply ooze charm. People can't say no to you; your powers of persuasion border on witchcraft!

Sometimes a person's Norn's Thread will form the shape of Sig (Figure 12.7). I knew a Gypsy palmist who refused to read the hand of anyone with this sign. When I told her that I wasn't afraid of it, she made a magick symbol in my direction and muttered something about me recklessly jeopardizing my soul's survival!

You can see that even practitioners of other traditions recognize this symbol as a most potent omen. Basically, it means this person will hit the world like a bolt of lightning; whether for good or evil depends on the individual. I once saw a print of the hand of Adolf Hitler, and right smack dab in the middle of his palm was the clearest Sig I ever saw. On the other hand, drawings of the hand of Michelangelo show a clear Sig also. When you see this sign, you know

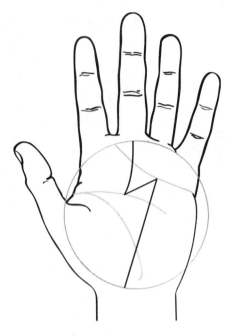

FIGURE 12.7—Norn's Thread in the
shape of Sig

you're in the presence of someone with the potential for greatness. Try and steer this person in the right direction!

Tyr's Eight

(Note: The discussions of Ehwaz, Manaz, and Daeg are found under "The Major Runes" on pages 149 and 150.)

Tyr: This is a very common and easy rune to spot and interpret. You have a strong competitive edge in the area indicated. You can beat out all your competitors and rise to the head of your profession—assuming you happen to be in the field where Tyr is found! For example, if Tyr is found under Loki and you work at a job where you are alone in a cubicle crunching numbers, you will not benefit from the power of the rune. You will find your greatest success in the fields of sales and communications.

 Beorc: This shows a family spirit in the area indicated. Whenever Beorc is found in a hand, the person will be a great humanitarian.

- If found under Odin, you are the sort of boss who treats employees like family. You feel personally responsible for those who work under you. Sadly, this kind of employer is rapidly becoming extinct! If you are not an employer, you will tend to adopt the people around you, becoming the surrogate parent of your group.

- If found under Hoenir, you see all of humanity as your spiritual family. You will work toward the betterment of humanity as a whole.

- If found under Bragi, your creative energies find their best expression within the family unit. For example, you always create memorable and exciting holiday events and family get-togethers.

- If found under Loki, you use your communication powers to help people.

 Lagu: This indicates sensitivity, empathy, intuition, and psychic energies. These energies are most effective in the area where Lagu is found.

- If found under Odin, you are good at making intuitive decisions in a crisis. A natural leader and hero, you instinctively know what to do when everyone else is running around in circles screaming their heads off. You act first, then think about the consequences later.

- If found under Hoenir, you are very psychic, often displaying a wide range of clairvoyance, empathy, and the ability to read others.

- If found under Bragi, your creativity will be more intuitive than logical. In other words, instead of blocking out a painting or planning an elaborate outline for a novel, you'll just jump in and instinctively make it up as you go along!

- If found under Loki, you will instinctively know what to say to people. You can be a real flatterer (one Loki told me she preferred to think of herself as a "positive motivator!"); you know just what people want to hear and can give it to them. If you're a salesperson, you will be able to read clients and provide them with exactly the product or service they need.

Ing: This is another rune possessing general energizing power. It shows the ability to produce results. It indicates creativity in a real or practical sense (as opposed to a dreamer). A very positive rune wherever found, you will make your mark on the world in the field indicated. If you are employed in another field, you cannot benefit from Ing's power and will be in constant danger of job dissatisfaction or burn-out.

Othel: This shows the area where your greatest earning power resides. If you enter the field where Othel is found, you will almost certainly make lots of money. Will you be happy? Look elsewhere for the answer to this question. Othel only deals with material issues! Othel can also indicate an inheritance, but not necessarily a monetary one. Sometimes it can hint at abilities or genetic traits inherited from parents that can be extremely useful and valuable if properly cultivated.

My goodness—another long write-up! Please take a rest before going to the next chapter. We're almost through!

Listen to my counsel, O King!
You will fare well if you follow it.
Never rise at night unless you need to spy,
Or to ease yourself in the Outhouse.

THE WORDS OF THE HIGH ONE

13

THREE
CASE HISTORIES

The lapse of ages changes all things—time, language, the
earth, the bounds of the sea, the stars of the sky, and every thing "about,
around, and underneath" man, except man himself.

LORD BYRON

At this point you have learned a great deal about the runic palmistry system, as well as a couple of ways to use the runes to answer questions. Now we'll see how this information flows together in the course of a reading.

Brian, Age 36

I selected this print because it contains more runes than any hand I've ever seen before. As you can see, Brian is a Heimdall type.

You will notice that Brian has the rune of Gifu (✕) under Bragi. This gives him a wonderful creative gift, but—uh, oh!—just above it is Neid (↑) blocking the Bragi energies. This shows that although he longs for creative expression, his present circumstances won't allow his talents to grow in that direction. Also,

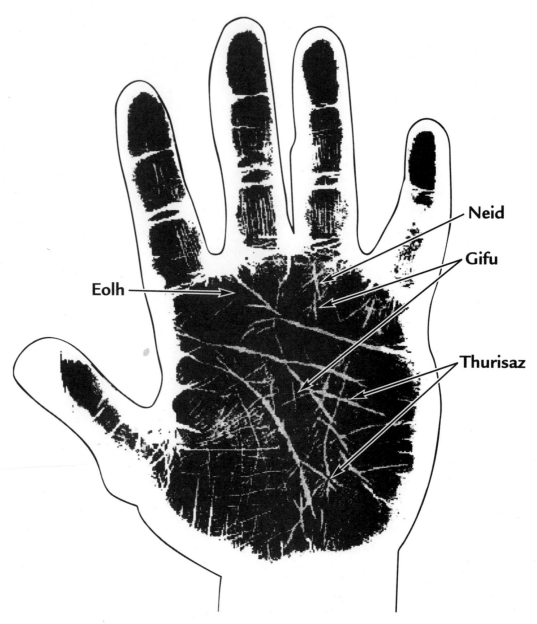

Neid

Gifu

Eolh

Thurisaz

FIGURE 13.1—Brian's hand

please observe the numerous appearances of Thurisaz (ᚦ), providing protective energies in certain areas of Brian's life. One appears on his Norn's Thread and another on his branch of Sif. The most fortunate sign on his hand is Eolh (ᛉ), at the end of his Freya's branch, denoting a happy and successful relationship that will last all of his life.

Here is the reading I gave Brian, condensed from its original one-hour length in order to touch on a few of the highlights:

"Brian, the first thing I look at is the overall shape of your hand, which tells us about your basic, instinctive approach to life. The shape of the hand represents the deep subconscious, so it tells us what is really pulling your strings below your conscious awareness. Do you understand?"

He nodded.

"You have what is known as a Heimdall or water hand, which basically shows me that you have a restless nature. You hate to have to sit still too long, waiting around for something to happen."

"That's true—I like to keep moving."

"All these lines in your hand show where your energy goes, and as you can see you tend to scatter yourself all over the place! It may be difficult for you to stay focused on one thing, because instead of going in a straight line or focusing on one thing, you generate a million tangents along the way. This makes life very interesting but will put a lot of mileage on you as you get older. You could probably benefit from a grounding influence of some kind, something like a solid relationship or job commitment that helps keep your feet on the ground.

"The long fingers show me that you're very sensitive to details, and are probably a bit of a perfectionist—"

"Right!"

"—and that you tend to be a bit critical of others [*note the angle of Aegir*]. But you're most critical of yourself [*Odin leaning toward Hoenir*], and, in my opinion, you underestimate yourself in key areas."

"What can I do about that?"

"Essentially, it's a matter of changing your internal programming. I'll show you how to do that in a minute." [*Note: Notice the Heimdall's desire to keep the information flowing. You can expect to be interrupted a lot by a water person!*]

"Brian, you're a person who prefers to achieve his ends diplomatically, avoiding confrontation. You thrive on harmony and peace, and avoid conflict. You like for things to flow smoothly. Peace and quiet are dear to your heart."

"Well, I'm a Libra." [*He also has a very long Bragi finger!*]

"Your hand contains a great many lines of dissatisfaction. This symbol under your ring finger is Gifu, a Norse rune symbolizing where your greatest gift can be found. When it's under your ring finger it means that you would be happiest in a creative field. Unfortunately, there are complications preventing you from doing this. This sign is called Neid, and indicates an unfulfilled yearning. From this, I can say that you would love to express your creative side, but for some reason or another you cannot.

"Your branch of Mimir shows a practical and logical mind, so you require practical solutions to your problems. We can do that. One of the biggest issues in your life can be spotted here. This is your Norn's Thread, which shows the development of your personality. It begins in an area known as the Void, which indicates you have an unusual, off-the-wall personality, almost mystical. Compared to the rest of your family unit, you may feel that you're from a different planet."

Brian laughed.

"You'll tend to test limits, and if I'm not mistaken, this is a no-no in your chosen field. You'll enjoy rolling the dice, adding improvements and variations, and rebelling against tradition. This can land you in hot water at work, I'm afraid."

"My supervisor always asks me why I can't just leave well enough alone."

"I'll bet. It's in your nature to question authority and test what you're told. This symbol is Thorn [*Thurisaz on the Norn's Thread*] and shows that you have put up defenses preventing anybody from getting too near to you. You keep people at arm's length until you know you can trust them. This is because, as we've already determined, you do not think like those around you. Even in a

room full of people you experience a sense of loneliness. These feelings of isolation will continue to plague you until you give yourself permission to express
who you really are, not what you think people want you to be."

Brian told me that he was an engineer, working for a company that manu-
factured tractors. He wasn't happy with his job (even though it paid very well)
and didn't know the source of his dissatisfaction. I answered that he needed
more freedom to express his creativity. After all, engineering is a very inflexible
discipline. He agreed.

"One of the most important signs in your hand is this big *M* in the middle.
You see that? In runic palmistry that is Manaz (ᛗ), which indicates you must
bring into your work a humanitarian element. I'll bet that you like to feel useful to others and go out of your way to work with people?"

"I coach on a little league team."

"And you probably get a lot of satisfaction out of that. One of the very good
signs in your hand is this trident formation at the end of Freya's branch [*Eolh*].
This branch governs your heart, and it predicts that you'll have a happy ending
to your romantic situation anyway."

"That's good news."

The reading continued in this direction for several minutes. "Now, I'd like
you to draw three runes from this bag and we'll try and get an overall picture of
your situation."

Brian drew Thurisaz, Manaz, and Gifu.

"All three of these runes appear in your hand, so they're especially significant. The Thorn appears in your past, which shows the defensive walls you've
put up in order to fit in with your situation. Unfortunately, you're in the
wrong situation, so these defenses, instead of protecting you, have become a
prison. They're trapping you in, instead of keeping others out."

"That's how I feel—like I'm trapped."

"You'll be able to escape, don't worry. You don't have to be Houdini to get out of traps of your own making! Manaz shows your present. In this case it shows the emerging of your humanitarian instinct in the present time, and so it's only natural that you're experiencing yearnings for a change in your life path. Now, the future is represented by Gifu, which shows the emergence of your gift—in your case, using your creative abilities to help humanity. This shows us that you will indeed learn to express this desire in real life. Please draw another rune to represent the outcome."

Brian drew again.

"This is good news. You drew Jera (ᛃ), which means that your time is about to come. Think of the four seasons; your winter is almost over and spring about to begin. But you must be brave—these things will not happen by themselves. You have to have the courage to make the changes that your heart so desperately craves. Can you do that?"

Brian assured me that he could. In fact, he had been looking into other employment opportunities back in his hometown. I gave him an amulet with the symbol Manaz carved on it to help him create the future he desired. I haven't heard from Brian since he moved, but I hope he was able to manifest all the happiness his reading revealed!

Brian's hand had a tremendous amount of information, including numerous other runes that weren't pertinent to the reading at that time. Practice searching for and interpreting these runes for your own enjoyment.

Evelyn, Age 48

Evelyn has a conic hand, with plenty of Heimdall (water) lines. You'll notice the most obvious rune in her hand is Ing (ᛜ), which you will find on her mount of Sif. Her Norn's Thread shows an unusual configuration. It's in the shape of Lagu (ᛚ). If you'll look closely under her Odin finger, you'll notice a faint Jera (ᛃ) rune. Since it's not very clear, however, the rune isn't completely active at the present time, so we won't mention it. The strongest branch on her hand is

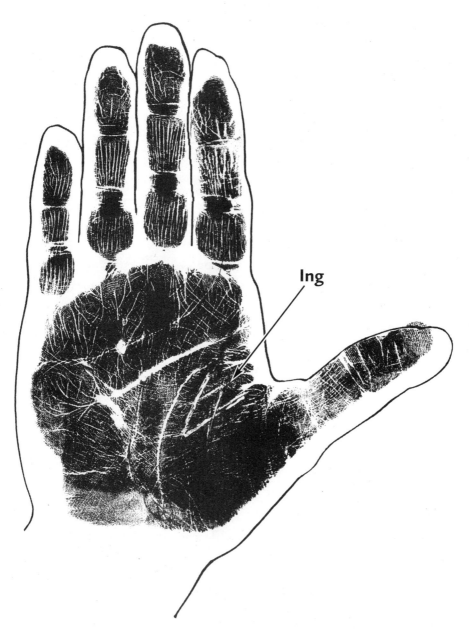

Ing

FIGURE 13.2—Evelyn's hand

Mimir's, showing her extremely active intellect. Eolh (Y) appears at the end of
Mimir, showing that she can generate extremely powerful thoughts and ideas.
Here are some of the highlights from the reading I gave Evelyn:

"Evelyn, you have a conic hand, which means you're extremely empathic.
Do you know what that means? It means that you're sensitive to the emotions
of others. This is a great gift if you're involved in a profession that helps people,
but in day-to-day life it can be a pain in the neck. It makes you attract people to
you who have a lot of problems."

She nodded in agreement, a rueful expression on her face.

"I sometimes call this the 'Dear Abby' hand, because you'll tend to attract
personal confessions from others, and people will always be asking you for
advice. At some point in your life you'll ask yourself why do all your friends
and family members have so many problems?"

"It's like a soap opera."

"Empathy can make your life very dramatic if you don't learn to say 'No'
sometimes. The problem with empathic people is that practically every time
they say 'Yes' it's for the wrong reasons. You probably have a strong sense of
personal responsibility for the well-being of others [*large, curved mount of
Nanna*], and if something's wrong with them, you feel it's your duty to fix
them. Am I right?"

"Yes you are."

"Fortunately, you have a very strong branch of Mimir, which means you
have a very active mind. You think and think about things, and since you have
long fingers you probably analyze people and things constantly. It's probably
hard for you to let go and relax at night and go to sleep. You go over every little
detail of your day and pick it to pieces. Because it's long, you may find you
resist change and hold on to a bad job or relationship longer than you really
should. It ends in a trident [*Eolh*], which shows that you have three ways of see-
ing things: the right way, the wrong way, and your way!" This cracked her up!
"The trident is a good omen because it blesses the area where it appears. In

your case, it's your mind that's blessed and you'll be able to generate excellent ideas that, if properly developed, could make you a lot of money.

"Your thumb tells me that you're quite stubborn [*her thumb was rigid*], and you tend to be outspoken [*notice the gap between Mimir and Sif!*]. You hate to be told you can't do something, and will defend your right to do exactly as you please. You may find that you tend to intimidate the more conservative men around you."

She laughed out loud. Later she told me this was her biggest problem at work. I hated to tell her that it was going to get worse the older she becomes! To continue:

"Your mound of Sif is large, which means you have a lot of vitality and can really get a lot of enjoyment out of life. Your resistance to disease is good and you have the internal power to throw off negative influences. You have the sign of Ing on Sif, so you probably have a lot of maternal energies. Combined with your empathy, this means that you tend to mother people, taking them under your wing. In this life, you may only have two or three children of your own, but you'll adopt the lost souls around you and make them your surrogate children."

We talked for a while about this tendency, which literally cluttered up her life with people who couldn't fend for themselves. We continued:

"Your branch of Freya, or heart line, is curved, showing you feel things deeply and show those feelings. It throws two forks: One fork goes under the second finger [*Eir's Twig*] and the other under the forefinger [*Frigg's Twig*]. This tells me that you tend to give and give to others. You love to have people around you and to help them, but at times you withdraw into yourself and want to be left alone. Ideally, the line should have a single ending between the fingers, but in your case you tend to go to emotional extremes which balance out over time."

Evelyn and I discussed her problems with getting along with others. She was a wild spirit, as evidenced by her Norn's Thread, and her spirit had chosen to be reincarnated into a strict, conservative family in order to learn to tame her wild spirit. Unfortunately, she spent most of her time and energies trying to rebel against her upbringing rather than incorporating the lessons in self-discipline she was meant to learn.

"Your Norn's Thread begins close to Sif, which shows that early in life you were most concerned with pleasing others. This is the time in your life where you tried to please everybody, and if they said they didn't like something about you, you would worry yourself to death over it. Now, you see how the thread swings out away from Sif? This means that the older you get, the less power other people have over you. Remember, your Freya branch shows that you tend to go to emotional extremes, so right now you're at the other end of the spectrum. You're at a point where you're saying, 'To heck with everyone else—I'll do what I want to!' Over time you'll balance out your drive for independence with your desire to be helpful to others. This may be the biggest lesson you have to learn in this life, so you can expect it to be the hardest."

It wasn't necessary to perform a runecast for Evelyn, since she really had no questions that weren't answered by the information in her palm. However, just for luck I had her draw a single rune. She drew Uruz (ᚢ).

"Evelyn, this rune represents the wild ox, but it can also mean a bull in a china shop! The message here is for you to avoid rushing in without first looking, to tame your wild energy, and put it to work for you instead of wasting it in conflict with others. You have to learn to only try and help people who are capable of helping themselves. This will be difficult, but once you begin to reap the rewards of your positive efforts, you'll wonder why you never did it before. Energy is neither good nor bad; it all depends on how you direct it. This rune is telling you that it's time to work toward your own good and let other people learn their own lessons."

Evelyn started her own business, which, interestingly enough, is a shelter for rescued stray cats! She's still saving others, but under her own terms now.

Elizabeth, Age 36

Now it's your turn! Here is Elizabeth's handprint. Study it for a moment, and then go on to the quiz. Good luck!

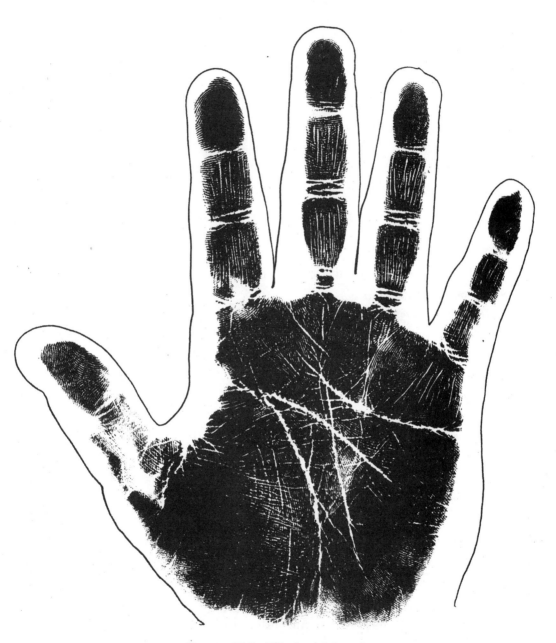

FIGURE 13.3—Elizabeth's hand

Quiz

1. What hand type is Elizabeth?
2. What major runes, if any, did you find?
3. What minor runes, if any, did you find?
4. Are her fingers long or short? (To determine length, measure the Odin finger from its tip to where Mimir's branch begins. If this distance is longer than the palm is wide, the fingers are considered long. If shorter, the fingers are considered short.)
5. Are Odin and Bragi in balance?
6. Is the branch of Freya curved or straight?
7. What can you tell from her thumb?
8. What can you tell from her Norn's Thread?
9. Is she a creative or technical thinker?
10. Is she a people person?

Answers

There are no right or wrong answers! Palmistry is an interpretive skill and you must learn to trust your instincts. However, here are a few hints:

1. Hand type: spatula-shaped palm with medium fingers.
2. Major runes: there's a big one in the center of the palm!
3. Minor runes: look between the Norn's Thread and Sif's branch near the heel of the hand. Also, what's that under her third finger? Be sure to carefully examine the end of Freya's branch!
4. Elizabeth's length of Odin is almost exactly the width of her palm, so she has neither long nor short fingers.
5. Lay a pencil across the tips of the fingers to determine if Odin and Bragi are in balance. Notice Elizabeth's Bragi is a trifle longer than Odin. What does this mean?
6. The Freya branch: a curved line ending in Eolh (Υ)—is this good or bad? Freya ends under Hoenir and shows Eir's Twig. What does this tell you about Elizabeth's relationship with people?

7. Her thumb: is the angle of Aegir wide or narrow? Is the tip of the thumb blunt or tapered? What does this mean?

8. The Norn's Thread begins in the Void. Will Elizabeth be conservative, or will she march to a different drum all her life? Will she feel that she fits in, or will she consider herself an outsider?

9. Mimir's branch is fairly straight, but does curve somewhat. She blends both technical and creative thinking, and for this reason would be a very talented designer.

10. The best hint here is the large mount of Nanna.

How did you do? I'll bet you did a marvelous job!

I see Earth rising a second time
Fair and green, out of the foam.
. . . At Idun's Field the Gods meet
To ponder again the Great Twilight
And the ancient Runes of the High Father.

THE SONG OF THE SYBIL

AFTERWORD

The last thing one discovers in composing a work is what to put first.

BLAISE PASCAL

The Norsemen knew that all things, even the heavens and the earth, must come to an end. Why should a book be any different? I've learned that reading a book and writing a book are the same in one respect: It's a journey. Thank you for traveling with me this far. You were an excellent companion!

I hope you've learned interesting things about yourself as we traveled together. Perhaps you gained a deeper understanding of your friends and family. Maybe you've been inspired to begin preparing yourself for a career as a palm reader. If you're an experienced reader, I hope you enjoyed looking at another way of reading the hand. In any case, I hope you had as much fun reading this book as I had writing it!

Take care, and may your higher power smile upon you all your days. See you in Valhalla!

Young and alone on a long road
Once I lost my way.
When I found another, I felt rich.
Man rejoices in Man.

THE WORDS OF THE HIGH ONE

THOR AND LOKI
AMONG THE GIANTS

Before leaving the Norsemen and their gods, let's have a final look at their rich mythic tradition. The following story was one of my grandmother's favorites.

The Journey to Utgard

Thor, the mighty thunder god, was bored. Nothing exciting had happened around Asgard for too long, so he decided it was time to pay the giants a visit. You could always rely on the giants to provide an interesting time.

Thor took with him his servant Thjalfi (*THEE-yal-fee*), and after some thought, decided to take along Loki the Trickster. "The giants are a cunning people," he reasoned. "Your tricks may be useful in dealing with them." Loki was bored too, so he was glad to tag along. The three set out toward Giantland on foot.

They had traveled far to the east when darkness fell. "Friends," said Thor, "there's no point in trying to go further tonight. Here we will make our camp."

The three were searching for a sheltered place to spend the night when Thjalfi called out, "We're saved! I've found a great hall!" Indeed, it was a large hall with a door as long as it was high. It appeared to be unoccupied. Going inside, the travelers discovered five long rooms. Thankful, they each retired to a separate room and prepared to sleep.

They were in for a restless time. All night long a ferocious storm boomed and blew outside and the weary travelers scarcely slept a wink. The earth quaked and the walls of the dwelling trembled. Loki and Thjalfi were terrified, but Thor stood watch all night, clutching his legendary hammer Mjollnir tightly in his large fist.

In the morning the three emerged from the hall to discover a sleeping giant sprawled out under a tree. "I believe I've located the source of the awful racket that entertained us through the night," Loki said. "It was that fellow's snoring." The giant, hearing their voices, woke up and greeted them.

"Good morning!" said he. "My, what small fellows you are. Have you seen my glove? Ah, there it is!" And with that he proceeded to pick up the hall in which the three had spent the night. What they thought were rooms had been the fingers of the giant's glove!

"What's your name, stranger?" asked Thor, who was never afraid of anyone, regardless of size.

"They call me Skryrnir [*SKRUR-ner*]," said the giant. "And there's no need to tell me who you are. I recognize you from stories I've heard. You're Thor. I would have thought you were bigger and stronger than you appear to be. Oh well, let's have breakfast." After breakfast, the giant agreed to journey with them to Utgard where the king of the giants made his home.

After walking many weary miles, Thor decided it was time for lunch. Skryrnir told them, "You go ahead and eat; here's the provision bag. I'm just going to take a nap under this tree." In a minute he was snoring loudly while Thor attempted to untie the knots on the provision bag.

But it was no use. The knots were so tight that even he, the strongest of the gods, couldn't open the bag. Nor could Loki, the most cunning being in all the world, figure out how to untie the devious knots. Overcome by rage and hunger, Thor strode over to the sleeping Skryrnir and smacked him in the head with Mjollnir, his mighty hammer.

Skryrnir rolled over and muttered something about a leaf falling on his head. Disgusted, Thor returned to his struggle with the bag. Incredible as it may seem, he couldn't get a single knot loosened. In frustration he hit the slumbering Skryrnir again, harder than before. Opening one eye, Skryrnir said, "I believe an acorn fell on my head. Have you finished supper yet?" Through gritted teeth, Thor replied that they were just going to go to sleep.

However, the frightful snores of the giant kept the three sufferers awake until Thor could stand it no more. Gripping Mjollnir firmly in both hands, he rang the hammer with every ounce of his strength against Skryrnir's head. The hammer sank in up to the handle. The giant woke up, rubbed his cheek, and remarked, "Must be some birds up in that tree. I swear they just knocked a twig down on my face. Thor, are you awake? You haven't far to go to reach Utgard. It's right over that hill there. You guys better be careful though. I overheard you whispering to yourselves last night about how big I am. Well, at Utgard you'll see some big men; compared to them I'm quite puny. You'd better mind your manners; the king isn't inclined to tolerate smart talk from little whippersnappers like you. Gentlemen, good day. I must part company with you as my business takes me elsewhere." Skryrnir threw the provision bag over his shoulder (and not a bite of food had Thor, Loki, or Thjalfi been able to extract from it), and whistling, strode off into the forest. None of the three travelers were sorry to see him go.

Loki whispered to Thjalfi, "We're in deep trouble if what that great oaf said is true. How can we hope to survive an encounter with beings more powerful than even Thor?" Thjalfi just shook his head, and the two followed Thor into Utgard.

The Hall of Utgard-Loki

Thor, Loki, and Thjalfi continued walking until around midday, when they arrived at the palace of Utgard-Loki, the king of the giants. The palace was magnificent; so tall that the top disappeared into the clouds. Although the gate was shut, the three managed to squeeze in between the bars. Looking around the vast property, they saw an enormous hall in the middle of the stronghold with doors wide open.

Thor in the lead, the three entered that amazing hall and walked toward the end of the room. Loki and Thjalfi cowered behind Thor for protection. On both sides of the hall a large number of men were seated feasting and drinking, and none of them were what you would call small. Presently they approached the powerful King Utgard-Loki who snorted contemptuously when he saw them.

"Unless I'm very much mistaken, this stripling who stands before me is the legendary Thor. All I can say is, you must be stronger than you look." Biting his lips, Thor said nothing. Turning his attention to Loki and Thjalfi the king said, "No one is allowed to stay among us unless he is a master of some craft or skill." His lip curled in scorn. "What is it that you can do to impress us?"

Loki immediately spoke up. "Sir, there is one outstanding accomplishment I have that no one can surpass: I can eat faster than any living being!"

Utgard-Loki stroked his beard and answered, "That's a remarkable claim if ever I heard one. We'll soon put it to the test." Utgard-Loki ordered a huge table of food prepared for the contest, and then called for his servant, a man called Loge. Loge sat at the north end of the table, Loki at the south, and at a signal both men fell to.

Loki's speed was enhanced by the fact that he hadn't eaten in several long days. But Loge wasn't far behind, and both men ate at an unparalleled pace. The large joints of meat seemed to disappear from the table by magic. When they met in the exact middle of the table, it was seen that Loki had eaten every scrap of meat, leaving nothing but bones. However, Loge had devoured meat, bones, and even his half of the table, so he was adjudged the winner!

"At least you got lunch out of the deal," Thjalfi muttered to the crest-fallen Loki.

Utgard-Loki turned to Thjalfi. "And what can you do, youngster? Hopefully you'll give us a better show than your companion."

Thjalfi replied, "Honored king, I can run faster than anyone alive. I would be willing to run a race against the champion of your choice." The king allowed that this was an impressive feat, if Thjalfi could make good his claim. A race course was set up and the king called for a lad named Hugi (*HYOO-gee*) to run against Thjalfi. They ran the race and Hugi was so far ahead that he was waiting at the finish line when Thjalfi came running up.

"You'll have to do better than that in the next race," sneered Utgard-Loki.

But try as he might, Thjalfi lost all three races to the incredibly fast Hugi, although the last race was nearly a tie. Loki said to him, "We're making a sorry spectacle of ourselves amongst these giants. I hope Thor can redeem our honor." Panting from his exertion, Thjalfi could only nod his head.

"My turn," roared the mighty Thor. "Give me a shot at the title, and I can assure you I'll serve you better than my companions."

"We'll see about that," replied Utgard-Loki.

Thor Accepts the Challenge

After Loki and Thjalfi were defeated by the king's champions, it was Thor's turn to show what he could do. Utgard-Loki asked, "And what do you have to show us, so-called Lord of Thunder? Men talk of your mighty deeds, so we're ready to be impressed—if you're up to the job."

Swallowing his anger at the king's scornful words, Thor answered calmly, "I would like nothing more than to pit myself against your champion drinker, for by Odin's eyeball I've worked up a mighty thirst listening to your bragging. I swear I can outdrink any man in Utgard!"

Utgard-Loki replied, "That may well be. We'll see." Calling for his cup-bearer, the king bade him fetch forth the horn from which his retainers were accustomed to drink. The cup-bearer handed Thor a drinking horn that was filled to the brim with foamy liquor. Utgard-Loki remarked, "We consider it average if a man can drain the horn in one gulp. The younger pups usually take two, and none but the elderly are so wretched as to require three drinks to see the horn's bottom."

Thor said, "Stand aside, and give me elbow room. I have a powerful thirst and I'll remove the arm of the man who stands between me and this horn." With that he placed the horn to his lips and began to drink. He drank in colossal gulps, the likes of which no one had ever seen before, and Thor thought to himself that victory was assured. But when he was forced to come up for air, he saw to his amazement that the level of liquid in the horn had hardly moved!

Utgard-Loki laughed and said, "Tsk, tsk. You drank well, but I would have expected better from the great Thor. No doubt you'll empty the horn with your second draught."

Thor rolled up his sleeves, loosened his belt, and, after belching loudly, committed himself to emptying that horn.

But alas! Although he had lowered the level a trifle more, Thor's second drink seemed insignificant compared to the amount of liquor remaining. "This cannot be!" he rumbled, and took a third drink, much longer and deeper than the previous two combined. When he looked in the horn again he had made a little more progress, but was nowhere near emptying it. The hall resounded with laughter, and Thor's face turned scarlet with rage.

"I would have thought better of you, Thor," said Utgard-Loki. "Perhaps our tests are just too hard. But there is another feat of strength you can attempt, if you wish."

"What's that?" Thor asked.

The king answered, "Well, it's really not much of a test. Actually, only children do it around here, but since you're faring so poorly it may appeal to you."

"What is it?" Thor shouted.

"Children perform the feat of lifting my old tomcat off the ground. It's not much of a test, as I said, and I would never have thought of offering such a thing to the great Thor, if I hadn't seen with my own eyes that you aren't as strong as I thought you were."

"Where's that accursed cat?" Thor demanded.

Thereupon a large gray cat jumped to the middle of the floor, meowing loudly. It was nothing unusual; perhaps a bit larger than the average specimen. Thor went over to it with a grim look on his face and began to lift. The cat refused to budge. Without another word Thor removed his shirt and began to push as hard as he could. He managed to position himself under the cat's belly and lifted with all his might. His sinews bulged like knots in an oak tree, but all he managed was to get one paw of the cat off of the ground.

Utgard-Loki addressed his men, saying, "Well, it is a rather large cat and Thor is a puny little fellow." Laughter rang throughout the hall. "Is there another trial you wish to attempt?" he asked sweetly.

Thor's face was purple with rage and embarrassment. "Now I'm really mad," he shouted. "Give me someone to wrestle! By Odin, I'll show you how little I am!"

The king agreed. "The problem is that looking about this hall at all these worthy men, I don't see anybody here who wouldn't consider it beneath him to wrestle with you. But wait, I have an idea! You can wrestle my foster mother, an old crone named Elli. Don't scoff—she's brought down stronger men than you, Lord of Thunder!"

Then an old woman tottered into the hall. To make a long story short, Thor wrestled with her to no avail. After a tremendous struggle, she eventually forced him down to one knee. Thor admitted he was badly beaten.

It was late into the evening, so the king bade the three guests to sit down for dinner. For the rest of the night he showed them splendid hospitality, although the spirits of the three guests were beyond cheering up.

The Next Morning

When dawn broke, the three disconsolate travelers prepared to return home. Utgard-Loki gave them a wonderful breakfast and nobody mentioned the humiliating events of the previous day.

After finishing the meal in silence, they set off to return to Asgard. King Utgard-Loki accompanied them to the forest. At the edge of his kingdom, the king asked Thor what he thought of his visit to Giantland.

Head held low, Thor replied, "I must admit you are the better man here, Utgard-Loki. Never have I suffered such awful defeats from anybody. My portion here was shame and defeat. What hurts worst of all is that now my name will become a laughingstock."

Utgard-Loki hesitated. Then he replied, "Thor, I will tell you the truth now that you are out of my house. And if I have any say in the matter, you'll never come here again. We had no idea of your terrible strength; you almost ruined us."

"What are you saying?" said Loki.

"You were defeated at my hands only through magick and spells. The first time I met you was in the woods. I tied up the provision bag with cords of solid iron, and you couldn't discover how to untie the magick knots. When you hit me in the head with your hammer those three times, I placed a mountain between you and me. You see that mountain over there?"

"Yes, so what?"

"Those two valleys are where your hammer fell the first two times. That great canyon in the middle is the result of your third blow. By my word, if any of those blows had landed on me, I would have been annihilated!"

"Hmmph," grumbled Thor.

"You were tricked by magick, son of Odin. The contests were rigged, too. Loki was hungry and ate faster than any mortal, but his opponent was none other than Wildfire, that which devours everything in its path!"

"By Odin's beard," whispered Loki. "I, the trickster—tricked!"

"What about me?" asked Thjalfi.

"Ah yes. My child, you were racing against my Thought, and nothing can be faster than that, although you came close."

"And the horn?" Thor demanded.

"Oh my word! That was the worst. The end of that horn was in the ocean, and by the time you finished your third drink, I feared you would drain the seabed dry! When you get to the ocean you'll see how much you depleted it. I never would have believed such a miracle was possible. And the cat you lifted was not what it appeared to be either; it was nothing less than the Midgard Serpent, which encircles the entire world and holds its own tail in its mouth. I thought we were demolished for sure when you managed to pry one of its paws from the ground! You stretched it so high it almost touched the very sky. Everyone who witnessed it was horrified. Such a feat has never been imagined."

"Hrummph," remarked Thor.

"What of the old crone?" asked Loki.

"This was the most amazing feat of all. She was really Old Age, against whom no man may win. Anyone who lives long enough will be tripped up by Old Age, and yet she was only able to force Thor down on one knee. Amazing!"

"Hah," Thor choked out, paralyzed with rage.

"And now, gentlemen, I must bid you farewell. Don't try to follow me. My magick will make sure you never stumble across my kingdom again. You're too powerful to allow into my home and you'll get no further victories at my expense. Good day."

Thor, recovering from his paralysis, grabbed his hammer to smash Utgard-Loki into smithereens. But when he whirled around, the giant king had vanished.

"Look," said Loki.

Where the giant's stronghold had been was now a sprawling plain of great beauty. Thor's knuckles were white as he gripped Mjollnir. He turned to his two companions and growled, "We shall never speak of this again—agreed?"

"Agreed."

But of course Loki did speak of it, and speak of it often—which is how the tale found its way into legend and song, and how we know of it to this day.

APPENDIᚷ

Runic Crib Sheet

A quick reference for your convenience!

Freya's Eight

ᚠ **Fehu** (*FEE-oo*): Positive omen. Cultivation of talent over time. Prosperity and wealth.

ᚢ **Uruz** (*OO-rooz*): Wild ox. An untamed sort of primal energy that promotes well-being and personal power. Uruz also helps you adjust to a sudden change. Symbol of independence and self-confidence.

ᚦ **Thurisaz** (*THUR-a-saz*): Symbol of protection. Like a thorn growing on a plant, it provides protection from attack.

ᚨ **Ansuz** (*AN-sooz* or *AN-sur*): Indicates an answer is forthcoming in the area indicated.

ᚱ **Raidho** (*RAY-tho*): Movement or travel of a spiritual or physical nature.

ᚲ **Ken** (*ken*): Knowledge, insight, psychic awareness.

ᚷ **Gifu** (*GIFF-oo*): A gift—either material or spiritual.

ᚹ **Wunjo** (*WUN-yo*): Exceptional luck; a windfall.

Hagall's Eight

ᚺ **Hagall** (*HAY-goll*): A blockage to progress that is out of your control.

ᚾ **Neid** (*rhymes with "hide"*): Dissatisfaction and frustrated desires.

ᛁ **Is** (*ice*): Frozen in time. Complete blockage of energy and movement.

⟨ **Jera** (*YER-ah*): Shows that the person's time is near. Talents and opportunities are emerging.

↓ **Yr** (*ear*): A powerful rune of protection. Eliminates obstacles and setbacks.

ᚲ **Perdhro** (*PERTH-ro*): Self-improvement, enlightenment, developing psychic abilities. Finding out hidden knowledge; learning secrets.

ᛉ **Eolh** (*EE-ol*): The most versatile symbol of protection. Eolh is a gentle, nurturing sort of energy.

ᚼ **Sig** (*sig*): A very aggressive symbol of power and protection. Use with caution!

Tyr's Eight

↑ **Tyr** (*tur*): Strength in competitive areas. Winning combat. Gaining the competitive edge.

ᛒ **Beorc** (*BEE-york*): Family and home. New beginnings.

ᛗ **Ehwaz** (*AY-waz*): Positive changes, often involving travel. Goals within reach.

ᛗ **Manaz** (*MON-ahz*): The rune of service to mankind. Humanitarianism.

ᛚ **Lagu** (*LAW-goo*): Indicates sensitivity, empathy, intuition, and psychic energies.

ᛜ **Ing** (*eeng*): Creativity, fertility, productivity.

ᛗ **Daeg** (*DAY-egg*): Optimism, a fresh start.

ᛟ **Othel** (*OH-thel*): Inheritance, material gain, inherited gifts. Also deals with a home or other type of structure.

Odin's Rune

Wyrd (*weird*): Related to the concept of karma or destiny; a mystery or unknown outcome. It's in the hands of fate!

BIBLIOGRAPHY

Aswynn, Freya. *Northern Mysteries and Magick.* St. Paul, Minn.: Llewellyn Publications, 1998.

Auden, W. H. (Wystan Hugh). *Norse Poems.* London: Athlone Press, 1981.

Crossley-Holland, Kevin. *The Norse Myths.* New York: Pantheon Books, 1980.

Dumézil, Georges. *Les Dieux des Germains.* Berkeley, Calif.: University of California Press, 1973.

Green, Roger Lancelyn. *Saga of Asgard: Myths of the Norsemen.* Illustrated by Brian Wildsmith. Philadelphia: Dufour Editions, 1964.

Greenway, John Langford. *The Golden Horns: Mythic Imagination and the Nordic Past.* Athens, Ga.: University of Georgia Press, 1977.

Mabie, Hamilton Wright. *Norse Stories Retold from the Eddas.* New York: Dodd, 1900.

Martin, John Stanley. *Ragnarok: An Investigation into Old Norse Concepts of the Fate of the Gods.* Assen: Van Gorcum, 1972.

Munch, Peter Andreas. *Norse Mythology, Legends of Gods and Heroes.* Translated by Sigurd Bernhard Hustvedt. New York: The American-Scandinavian Foundation, 1926.

Oxenstierna, Eric Carl Gabriel. *The Norsemen.* Translated and edited by Catherine Hutter. Greenwich, Conn.: New York Graphic Society Publishers, 1965.

Page, R. I. (Raymond Ian). *Norse Myths.* Austin, Tex.: University of Texas Press, 1990.

Rydberg, Viktor. *Teutonic Mythology: Gods and Goddesses of the Northland.* Translated by Rasmus B. Anderson. London: Norrœna Society, 1906.

Turville-Petre, Gabriel. *Myth and Religion of the North: The Religion of Ancient Scandinavia.* New York: Holt, Rinehart and Winston, 1964.

Other Books on Palmistry

Cheiro (Count Louis Hamon). *Palmistry for All.* New York: Arco, 1982.

Dukes, Terence. *Chinese Hand Analysis.* York Beach, Maine: Samuel Weiser, 1984.

Gettings, Fred. *The Hand and the Horoscope.* London: Trune Books Ltd., 1974.

Gibson, Litzka Raymond. *How to Read Palms.* Hollywood, Fla.: Lifetime Books, 1997.

Hipskind, Judith. *Palmistry: The Whole View*. St. Paul, Minn.: Llewellyn Publications, 1992.

Webster, Richard. *Revealing Hands*. St. Paul, Minn.: Llewellyn Publications, 1994.

Other Books About Runes

Kaser, R. T. *Runes in Ten Minutes*. New York: Avon Books, 1995.

Line, David, and Julia Line. *Fortune-Telling by Runes*. Wellingborough, Northamptonshire: The Aquarian Press, 1984.

Peschel, Lisa. *A Practical Guide to the Runes*. St. Paul, Minn.: Llewellyn Publications, 1993.

Willis, Tony. *Discover Runes: Understanding and Using the Power of Runes*. New York: Sterling Publishing Company, 1986.

INDEX

 REACH FOR THE MOON

Llewellyn publishes hundreds of books on your favorite subjects!
To get these exciting books, including the ones on the following pages,
check your local bookstore or order them directly from Llewellyn.

Order by Phone
- Call toll-free within the U.S. and Canada, 1-800-THE MOON
- In Minnesota, call (651) 291-1970
- We accept VISA, MasterCard, and American Express

Order by Mail
- Send the full price of your order (MN residents add 7% sales tax) in U.S. funds, plus postage & handling to:

  Llewellyn Worldwide
  P.O. Box 64383, Dept. 1-56718-577-0
  St. Paul, MN 55164–0383, U.S.A.

Postage & Handling
- **Standard** (U.S., Canada, & Mexico)

If your order is:
    $20.00 or under, add $5.00
    $20.01–$100.00, add $6.00
    Over $100, shipping is free

(Continental U.S. orders ship UPS. AK, HI, PR, & P.O. Boxes ship USPS 1st class. Mex. & Can. ship PMB.)
- **Second Day Air** (Continental U.S. only): $10.00 for one book + $1.00 per each additional book
- **Express** (AK, HI, & PR only) [Not available for P.O. Box delivery. For street address delivery only.]: $15.00 for one book + $1.00 per each additional book
- **International Surface Mail:** Add $1.00 per item
- **International Airmail:** Books—Add the retail price of each item; Non-book items—Add $5.00 per item

Please allow 4–6 weeks for delivery on all orders.
Postage and handling rates subject to change.

Discounts
We offer a 20% discount to group leaders or agents. You must order a minimum of 5 copies of the same book to get our special quantity price.

Free Catalog

Get a free copy of our color catalog, *New Worlds of Mind and Spirit.* Subscribe for just $10.00 in the United States and Canada ($30.00 overseas, airmail). Many bookstores carry *New Worlds*—ask for it!

Visit our website at www.llewellyn.com for more information.

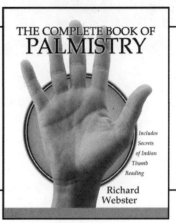

The Complete Book of Palmistry

Includes Secrets of Indian Thumb Reading

RICHARD WEBSTER

Formerly titled *Revealing Hands*.

The ability to read palms can lead you to a better understanding of yourself, as well as the complex motivations of other people. Now you can learn to advise others in a sensitive and caring manner, determine compatibility between couples, and help people decide what type of career suits them best.

As soon as you complete the first chapter, you can begin reading palms with confidence and expertise. Professional palmist and teacher Richard Webster leads you step-by-step through the subject with clear explanations and sample scripts that serve as a foundation for your readings for others. He answers all of the questions asked by his students over the years. Whether you are interested in taking up palmistry professionally or just for fun, you will find the information in this book exceptionally entertaining and easy to use.

1-56718-790-0
314 pp., 7½ x 9⅛, 174 illus. $14.95

Northern Mysteries & Magick
Runes, Gods, and Feminine Powers

FREYA ASWYNN

Formerly titled *Leaves of Yggdrasil*. Now revised and expanded. Includes the CD "Songs of Yggdrasil" and a bookmark of the runes.

The runes are more than an ancient alphabet. They comprise a powerful system of divination and a path to the subconscious forces operating in your life. *Northern Mysteries & Magick* is the only book of Nordic magick written by a woman, and it is the first to offer an extensive presentation of rune concepts, mythology, and magickal applications inspired by Dutch/Friesian traditional lore. Discover how the feminine Mysteries of the North are represented in the runes, and how each of the major deities of Northern Europe still live in the collective consciousness of people of Northern European descent. Chapters on runic divination and magick introduce the use of runes in counseling and healing.

Northern Mysteries & Magick emphasizes the feminine mysteries and the function of the Northern priestesses. It unveils a complete and personal system of the rune magick that will fascinate students of mythology, spirituality, psychism, and Teutonic history, for this is not only a religious autobiography but also a historical account of the ancient Northern European culture.

1-56718-047-7
288 pp., 6 x 9, with 40-minute CD $19.95

The New Palmistry
How to Read the Whole Hand and Knuckles

JUDITH HIPSKIND

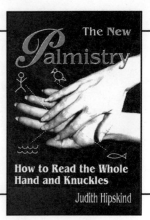

Ten years ago professional palmist Judith Hipskind make a shocking discovery. On the back of a client's hand, and in the knuckles specifically, she saw lines and symbols that revealed as much—if not more—than the palm lines she had studied for some fifteen years. Over the next decade, Hipskind researched the knuckles and received verification from hundreds of surprised and satisfied clients on the remarkable accuracy of her amazing new system.

In this groundbreaking book, Hipskind shares her discoveries so you, too, can easily read the secrets in the whole hand. We all know our future, and the subconscious mind records its information through the nerve supply to the knuckles. Your own hands contain incredibly clear answers to your questions about the immediate future of your career, finances, relationships, and health. Learn about the people in your life—significant others, your boss, or the person in the office next to you. Discover whether or not there will be difficulties ahead that can be worked out with advance warning, and find out whether your current efforts are leading to success.

1-56718-352-2
336 pp., 5¼ x 8, color photos $12.95

Palm Reading for Beginners
Find Your Future in the Palm of Your Hand

Richard Webster

Announce in any gathering that you read palms and you will be flocked by people thrilled to show you their hands. When you are have finished *Palm Reading for Beginners,* you will be able to look at anyone's palm (including your own) and confidently and effectively tell them about their personality, love life, hidden talents, career options, prosperity, and health.

Palmistry is possibly the oldest of the occult sciences, with basic principles that have not changed in 2,600 years. This step-by-step guide clearly explains the basics, as well as advanced research conducted in the past few years on such subjects as dermatoglyphics.

1-56718-791-9
264 pp., 5³⁄₁₆ x 8, illus. $9.95

Instant Palm Reader
A Road Map to Life

LINDA DOMIN

Etched upon your palm is an aerial view of all the scenes you will travel in the course of your lifetime. Your characteristics, skills, and abilities are imprinted in your mind and transferred as images onto your hand. Now, with this simple, flip-through pictorial guide, you can assemble your own personal palm reading, like a professional, almost instantly.

The *Instant Palm Reader* shows you how your hands contain the picture of the real you—physically, emotionally, and mentally. More than 500 easy-to-read diagrams will provide you with candid, uplifting revelations about yourself: personality, childhood, career, finances, family, love life, talents, and destiny.

With the sensitive information artfully contained within each interpretation, you will also be able to uncover your hidden feelings and unconscious needs as you learn the secrets of this 3,000-year-old science.

1-56718-232-1
288 pp., 7 x 10, illus. $14.95

Spanish edition:
Interprete sus manos

1-56718-930-X $12.95

To order, call 1-800-THE MOON
Prices subject to change without notice

Rune Magic

Donald Tyson

Drawing upon historical records, poetic fragments, and the informed study of scholars, *Rune Magic* resurrects the ancient techniques of this tactile form of magic and integrates those methods with modern occultism so that anyone can use the runes in a personal magical system. For the first time, every known and conjectured meaning of all thirty-three known runes, including the twenty-four runes known as "futhark," is available in one volume. In addition, *Rune Magic* covers the use of runes in divination, astral traveling, skrying, and on amulets and talismans. A complete rune ritual is also provided, and twenty-four rune words are outlined. Gods and goddesses of the runes are discussed, with illustrations from the National Museum of Sweden.

0-87542-826-6
224 pp., 6 x 9, photos $12.95

Norse Magic

D. J. CONWAY

The Norse: adventurous Viking wanderers, daring warriors, worshippers of the Aesir and the Vanir. Like the Celtic tribes, the Northmen had strong ties with the Earth and elements, the gods and the "little people."

Norse Magic is an active magic, only for participants, not bystanders. It is a magic of pride in oneself and the courage to face whatever comes. It interests those who believe in shaping their own future, those who believe that practicing spellwork is preferable to sitting around passively waiting for changes to come.

The book leads the beginner step by step through the spells. The in-depth discussion of Norse deities and the Norse way of life and worship set the intermediate student on the path to developing his or her own active rituals. *Norse Magic* is a compelling and easy-to-read introduction to the Norse religion and Teutonic mythology. The magical techniques are refreshingly direct and simple, with a strong feminine and goddess orientation.

0-87542-137-7

240 pp., mass market, illus. $4.99

The Rites of Odin

ED FITCH

The ancient Northern Europeans knew a rough magic drawn from the grandeur of vast mountains and deep forests, of rolling oceans and thundering storms. Their rites and beliefs sustained the Vikings, accompanying them to the New World and to the steppes of Central Asia. Now, for the first time, this magic system is brought compellingly into the present by author Ed Fitch.

This is a complete source volume on Odinism. It stresses the ancient values as well as the magic and myth of this way of life. The author researched his material in Scandinavia and Germany, and drew from anthropological and historical sources in Eastern and Central Europe.

A full cycle of ritual is provided, with rites of passage, magical spells, divination techniques, and three sets of seasonal rituals: solitary, group, and family. *The Rites of Odin* also contains extensive "how-to" sections on planning and conducting Odinist ceremonies, including preparation of ceremonial implements and the setting up of ritual areas. Each section is designed to stand alone for easier reading and for quick reference. A bibliography is provided for those who wish to pursue the historical and anthropological roots of Odinism further.

0-87542-224-1
360 pp., 6 x 9, illus. $14.95

Coin Divination
Pocket Fortuneteller

RAYMOND BUCKLAND

If you've ever flipped a coin to help you make a decision, you've already practiced the art of divination, or fortunetelling. Now, for the first time, a book is available that shows you how to expand on the art of coin divination so you can examine your present and future anytime, anywhere.

From the simplest single coin toss to the more complicated *I Ching* and tarot readings, you will learn how to answer any question or shed light on any dilemma, whether it involves career, love, family, money, or health.

The coins are waiting to speak to you. See which method appeals to the fortuneteller within:

- Use a single coin, two, three, or more
- Use a coin as a planchette of a talking board
- Use a deck of cards with your coins for more in-depth readings
- Work with five coins to conduct a revealing numerology reading
- Add an interesting twist to your readings by combining the coins with astrology, tarot, dominoes, or the *I Ching*
- Make your divinations more powerful by consecrating the coins, making your own coins, or personalizing existing coins

1-56718-089-2
240 pp., 5¾₆ x 6, illus. $9.95